Jordan,

To my friend wh [♡ S0-BZG-285] d.

It was my hope to write a "timeless" book. Something you read today and re-read at a later time in your life and get a different

WISDOM OF A LIFETIME

THINGS I WOULD WANT YOU TO KNOW
IF I DIED TOMORROW

message. I hope that's how it is for you.

By

Joseph Assante

You are the kind of girl that a person could surrender their soul to. It's not just your outer beauty but you have an attractive inner complexity that some would want to spend an eternity exploring. That may not make sense to you, a lot like hearing your own voice recorded. You don't think its you but it is. The message is, be gentle with other people's hearts you are easy to fall in love with.

ISBN: 1-4107-1775-5 (e-book)
ISBN: 1-4107-1774-7 (Paperback)

This book is printed on acid free paper.

1stBooks – rev. 03/10/03

TABLE OF CONTENTS

DEDICATED TO EVERYONE I CONSIDER FAMILY...
TO KIERAN AND KEATON, WITH LOVE,
AND TO DEBBIE, MY WIFE,
WHOSE LOVE AT FIRST SIGHT HAD ENOUGH VISION
TO LAST A LIFETIME

INTRODUCTION

In August 1999, an insurance man came to our newly purchased house to provide us with insurance, so in the event that one of us dies, our family will be provided for.

This started me thinking about my death. I was thirty years old and in decent health, but sometimes accidents happen and good health is irrelevant. The insurance policy would help cover our family's financial needs, but what about you growing up without knowing your Dad?

Your Mom and I had known each other since February 1985. If you do the math, that was half of my current life. She knew me better at that time, than most people and if you approached her ten years after my death and asked her how she thought I would handle a certain situation, she would have given you an answer seventy-five percent of the time that would have been, a hundred percent accurate. I am writing this book for the other twenty-five percent of the time when she may not have known how I would have thought or reacted to a certain situation.

To many people, this book may seem strange or macabre, but I can assure you it has reason for existence. I can easily picture a man of my age on his deathbed with only minutes to live. A horrified look is on his face, not from his life threatening injury, but from the realization that there are things he will never get to tell his children. Either they were not old enough to understand or because things never came up or just because he was always working and never made the time to have a heart to heart chat about life with his kids.

If only he could have more time. If only he had written things down that he wanted to pass along. A chance to explain why life is the way it is as he sees it, not as others may have believed he saw it. Perhaps if he wrote his ideas down when he had time to focus on his thoughts and review them so they read the way he meant them. So many times life puts us in situations where we are distracted while trying to focus. The words that leave our mouths are not the words we would have really wanted to say if given the correct atmosphere to consider them. So we collect our thoughts, focus, and say what is in our hearts to make things right. If we had died one minute before the words had been spoken, you would spend an eternity wishing for that one minute back.

This book doesn't give death the satisfaction. My children will know the truth. If a question does come up that I have not answered by this book it is not that I was trying to avoid any subject or fact, it is just that I probably did not think of it when I wrote the book. It is my hope that this book will inspire others to follow in my footsteps…

CHAPTER I

ABOUT ME

This topic is one of the more difficult ones to write about because it forces me to self analyze myself.

The premise of this book is that I am dead and that you kids are looking for answers, not only who I was, but what were my strengths and weaknesses. Chances are, we would have shared those same strengths and weaknesses.

I was born on September 24, 1969, in East Orange, New Jersey. At the age of three and a half I was adopted and brought to Martinsville. It should be noted that I have always considered the people who raised me to be my true parents. In your lives, you are going to encounter people who are adopted who insist on finding their biological parents. I have always believed that if the biological parents wanted to find their children they had to put up for adoption, they would do the looking, and if it was meant to be, their search would be successful. The biggest question that I think adopted people want answered is, "Why were things so bad that you opted to have me put up for adoption?" I always thought it would have been cool that the parents who adopt a child should receive a letter from the biological parents that gives the details of what brought this child to this place in life. Now that the Internet is a part of everyday life, there is no excuse why a biological parent could not post an explanation of what happened. Maybe they could include a picture and a number for contact in case the person who was adopted wants to discuss things further. Or maybe, the adopted person can post a note saying, "In case you are wondering, I am alive and well and I do not hold a grudge." This will give their biological parents a little piece of mind. I knew a mom who had to put her child up for adoption. She used to think about her now adopted child all the time and wonder if she was all right. I had actually sent this idea off to Dave Thomas at Wendy's. He too was adopted and has tried to help others in all related areas of adoption. If anyone could make a website like this a reality, he could.

1

Personally, the only circumstances in which I would meet my biological parents would be if the parents who raised me, introduced them to me. In my mind, it is the only appropriate forum. Any other way, I'd feel as if I betrayed my present parents.

I have always had a tremendous recollection about my life before the age of three. I remember the woman's face that took care of me. I remember playing with a boy quite frequently. His name was Ron. I called him Ronald McDonald. I think he was my brother, although I have been told otherwise.

On the day I was adopted I remember being dressed in a blue and red T-shirt with a little sailboat on it with matching sailboat shorts. "Stand up straight", I was told. "Do not forget to smile and do not forget your bag", I was ordered. I left with the clothes on my back and a paper bag that contained what was supposed to be three of my favorite toys. I took a teddy bear, a little stuffed puppy whose neck had no stuffing so his head would wobble from side to side, (my favorite) and a third toy.

The third toy changed my life. It was a shiny racecar. It was Ron's favorite toy. I had actually never played with it, but when Ron did, it seemed to sparkle. I got taken before he did, so it was mine to take. Those were the rules. I will never forget Ronald being dragged out of the playroom screaming and crying. I could hear his wails of agony from having lost his favorite toy.

When I got to my new home, I was brought to my room and as soon as I had a moment alone, I dumped out the contents of the bag. I propped my animals up on my pillow and proceeded to play with Ron's car. No matter what I did, I could not make it sparkle like Ron did. I could only hear his screams echoing in my head. I put the car in my drawer and never played with it again. I vowed from that day forward to never be selfish or greedy again. I have done what I could to make it hold true, even today.

I am going to fill you in on significant things that happened in my life that helped shape me today. I am tremendously honest about everything. Unlike most men in general, I am not afraid to admit I have flaws. This is something I have evolved into. I cannot speak for women, but most men spend a better part of their lives attempting to live up to unrealistic ideals that either society places on them or that they conjure up themselves. Then one day the realization hits you that you aren't all things to all people or God's gift to society and that you have some pretty real insecurities that you need to come to grips with.

The problem for me arises when I have to co-exist in a room with men who have yet to make the transition from Mr. Macho, are you talking to me, my penis is bigger than yours, Neanderthal, to a regular guy, a girl would bring home to mom. Some guys figure it out later in life after they lose their looks, others never get the point, and die in hospitals taking swings at the nurses.

The sooner you can come to grips with your imperfections, the more honesty seeps into your everyday life. You learn to accept your limitations and excel with your strengths. Best of all, you get to know the true meaning of love. It is a process that can open the darkest heart, and without getting too mushy, it's wonderful.

If anyone asked me a question about myself, I would give that person an honest answer. Some people find it refreshing, others disturbing. Believe it or not, some people prefer not to hear the truth. The saying goes, "Ignorance is bliss". It is as if the truth doesn't exist if they don't know about it. We live in a world where people don't want to know about other people's shortcomings, unless it is on a daytime talk show. Just maybe if we all put down our shields of defense, we all would see that we share similar weaknesses, but it will never happen because of fear. Fear is the most crippling thing you are going to face in your life. I have made great strides in overcoming my fears, and it started with being honest with myself, and those around me.

A word of caution about what you think versus what you say. I have always had a decent perception of the way things are. The problem has come up when I voiced my perceptions. I have always had a sharp tongue. Nothing is more permanently damaging than the spoken word. Wounds heal, scars fade, but the words of another person can cause a pain that can never be taken back or unspoken. You may not like a person for one reason or another, but I wouldn't be surprised if you trace backwards in their lives to find a defining moment where someone said something to them that set the tone for the rest of their life. Unable to shake off the comment, the person then becomes consumed by the other person's words and proceeds to live out the ideas and thoughts that he or she is now branded with. Learn from my mistakes; think before you speak.

From my earliest recollection I absolutely adored females. I used to get in fights with another boy in nursery school because I wanted to have naptime next to a cute girl.

My Dad often revisits the day I was adopted. I was three and a half years old and sitting on the lap of a big-breasted blonde social worker, stroking her breasts. Every time she removed my hand, I would look up at her, smile, and continue fondling until she finally gave in and let me continue.

Some boys, early in life, don't want to be around girls. Unlike other boys, I grew up with a keen insight and perception that other boys are deprived of. It wasn't that I played with dolls. I just grew up appreciating the sights, sounds and scents of women.

My primary companion growing up was my cousin Linda. I remember the first time we met. Our families had bought us "Big Wheels" and we were driving down my Uncle's driveway. I, of course, rolled mine over within two minutes. I scraped up my leg and was crying. Linda came over to me, picked me up and kissed my cheek. From that point on we were inseparable.

At about age twelve, I started to notice my parents "preferred" we not spend as much time together as we did. I think our parents thought we were fooling around with each other. From age six I wanted to do something but I was too young to know what. At age ten I knew what I wanted to do but couldn't follow through. I always fantasized that some day we would get married. I figured it would be cool for her because her last name wouldn't change. I loved her in every way possible a ten year old could. We had an amazing bond that I didn't want to ruin by attempting to make a move on her. Linda taught me something many men just never learn, how to respect females.

Out of frustration that I couldn't be with Linda I began making moves on all her friends. This became a sore point between us and when she confronted me about it, I couldn't give her a straight answer as to why I was doing it. It was only recently at my Uncle's July

Fourth party that it became clear. Her husband reminds me of me. We share some similar qualities. I overheard a comment that was made that he and I could be brothers, which made me flash back to a comment about your Mom and Linda passing for sisters. Unconsciously, we picked mates with similar qualities.

At the age of thirteen and all years after that Linda became a thorn in my side. It wasn't her fault. She was exceptional at sports and academics. She was everything I wasn't. My parents and teachers constantly forced me into her shadow. It seemed like anyone I met or spoke to at some point ended the conversation with, "Why can't you be more like your cousin Linda?"

As we got older our families did less and less with each other. I never resented Linda for her strengths, if anything she helped me become a better person. And the last friend of hers I ended up hitting on was your Mom. So, without Linda, I wouldn't have you guys.

In trying to figure what factors help shape me, I can't help but to factor in a local radio station I woke up with every morning. They played a few minutes from comedy albums every morning. These "laugh trax" as they were called helped me start my day with a smile. To this day I can recite some of those routines from twenty years ago.

I have a dry sense of humor. I grew up watching too much TV. One of my favorite shows was M.A.S.H. On the show, the main character, Hawkeye (played by Alan Alda), used to look at the reality of life and point out its humorous contradictions. Growing up I did all I could do to mimic his delivery of material.

Whenever I was in trouble and grounded from TV, I sought refuge from MAD Magazine. Satire is another form of dry comedy and I did all I could to look at life and laugh. I never liked reading actual books because it never held my attention. In fact, I have only read one fiction book cover to cover. The book was called, "Illusions" by Richard Bach. It is a must read. I do enjoy reading and learning from educational material although I wouldn't exactly describe myself as anything but mechanically declined. Usually if I touch something it breaks with very little hope of it ever working again.

In my life I have held many jobs. Most of the time I applied for jobs that would improve an existing flaw. For example, not being particularly mechanical, I went to work at a gas station just to be

5

around cars more often so I wasn't so helpless with them, and the list goes on and on.

I have been uncertain about picking a solid career my whole life. I know the secret for picking a career but it was not until recently that I understood it. The catch phrase is "find something you love to do and get paid for it". Ever since I was old enough to be asked, "What do you want to be when you grow up?" I have answered, "A professional stuntman". What better job could you ask for? You jump off a building and get paid a lot of money to boot. What fun! I had always imagined myself as a loner. I didn't like myself much and I never imagined anyone else would either. I decided it wouldn't be fair to another person to put my life on the line daily so I gave up on the whole idea. So then I started on this rampage where I picked careers for the sole purpose of trying to make a lot of money. I went to college for marketing because I heard good money was there. I have pursued computer schools and even learned to drive a tractor - trailer all in hopes of making a big killing and I never did. It actually is a point of interest that astounds me because I have never had a love for money. It was always the people around me making it a factor. Society puts too much self worth on being rich. Some people actually kill themselves because they do not have money and kill others because they do. Money's affect on people is a real sickness and I was not sure that I wouldn't fall into the same trap. Anyone can make a pay check. You are as valuable as you think you are. A tall order in today's world where it seems every one is a millionaire but you.

I have come to the realization that I have been unable to find anything I love to do because up until a short time ago I was incapable of loving myself. I know now why this occurred. In the past I have had no idea what it meant to have gratitude for what I had. I never appreciated what life gave me. People used to ask me how I was and my response was, "Well... I'm not dead". In reality that was a lie. In many respects I was dead to the world. I was an ingrate. I did not appreciate what life was.

Without being grateful for what you have, you never take stock in what you have. If you never take stock in what you have, you may waste your energy striving to either get something you already have or something that you really do not need. I am not only talking about physical possessions. I am talking about everything in your life. Health, love and the ability to take a breath are our greatest possessions.

I think I have spilled my guts enough about who I am and what shaped me. Other details about me will surface in future chapters. The next two chapters I wrote with each child in mind. The words on the pages will reflect a private conversation between you and I, but I want you to read each other's chapters. It may provide you with insight on what pitfalls I believe may come your way. I am writing this book to cover details of questions you might have wanted me to answer about myself, and life in general. The premise is that I am dead now, so I can only answer the questions you have via this book. So, if it seems like I veer off a lot, it is because I am trying to be thorough.

CHAPTER II

TO KIERAN

At some point, the question is going to come up why you were named Kieran. Until you become a parent you may not understand that picking out a name for your child is one of the toughest before birth challenges there ever was.

Kieran comes from Gaelic Irish and does not translate into anything poetic. Your name spoken aloud, in India, means ray of light. Your Mom and I thought it sounded cool.

The reason it is so difficult to name a child is this: Children can be cruel. They will take a child's name and twist it and poke fun at it in a mean spirited attempt to pass the time. It is a part of growing up and the more anyone sees it bothers you the more relentless the name calling gets.

I spent most of seventh grade attempting to come up with a new first name for myself. I have always liked the letter "K". If for no other reason, they are fun to draw. I came up with Kier, which I deliberately mispronounced "key-air" using two syllables. It was really pronounced just Kir, one syllable. We finally settled on Kieran.

I feel as if I could write for years on things I would want you to be advised about. Let's focus on three things that as a man are prone to cause you ninety-five percent of life's ups and downs; women, money and substances. I will start with what I feel is the easiest of the three.

When I say substances, I am referring to anything you can ingest that will alter your senses. Since the age of fifteen, I have not ingested the slightest bit of alcohol. I have even gone to the extreme of avoiding alcohol in foods and medicines. While this may seem a bit extreme to some people, I have good reason. Genetically speaking, I do not know my history. In your life you are going to hear the term "genetically predisposed". This refers to a person's susceptibility to a disease or action being higher due to a family history of said problem somewhere down the line. The person already has the flaw coded into their genes and with the proper stimulation, the code will be cracked and the problem will surface. That is not to say that the problem cannot be avoided completely if the stimulus is not present. However, it may manifest itself in other ways. For example, a person may have alcoholic tendencies due to a genetic weakness, and is never exposed to alcohol, may be more uniquely affected by a subtle drug like nicotine or caffeine. This is only my opinion and is not based on any scientific fact that I am aware of. I learn things by observation. Learn to pay attention to details. Life's greatest lessons can be learned by listening and not by talking.

You can witness for yourself how substance abuse devastates lives and families. People lose their jobs because they cannot go to work without drinking or doing drugs.

Historically, my parents grew up watching TV shows where the first thing the dad did after he got home after a hard days work was fix himself a drink. My generation seems to watch anything that goes on TV. As you grow, I suspect your generation will find even more creative ways to temporarily alter your brain's chemistry to give you that "high feeling".

What it comes down to is self -abuse due to low self- esteem. It has been my observation that if people are genuinely happy with their own lives, they don't abuse themselves with temporary fixes. They have great lives with no time for such abuses and they have better things to do with their lives. They are focused enough that they wouldn't waste the precious time getting drunk or high. The point is, that at some point in your life if you feel the need to smoke or drink, it should be a red flag for you that something is wrong with your life. Think before it happens to you.

I was once told, that money was the essence of life from which all happiness stems from. I have also met people that say money is unimportant and family and love is everything. Add to the mix the old saying that "too much of anything is no good" and you are nothing but good and confused on the topic.

I have never had a great deal of money. I can tell you what I have seen it do to other people. Money causes people to lose a sense of who they are. More than once I have seen families who win the lottery have their lives ruined by it. Yet, it is the American dream to

9

win it. Husbands and wives kill each other for insurance money. Politicians shape laws for people who donate to their campaigns. Money becomes a sickness for many people. It becomes a want that never gets fulfilled because you always want more.

The problem lies with the fact that people cannot distinguish between what they want and what they need. They have three cars but they want a fourth. They have two homes but they want one in every state. They have a false notion that this will make them happy, when in reality they have no idea what would make them happy. I have always believed it was wrong to want for more than you need.

Possessions seem to make you lose sight of who you really are. You lose your identity because you find out the thing you want badly really owns you because you will do anything to get it, including compromise what would normally be your solid values. There is a saying, "You can't con an honest man." It means if you live your life on the side of honest values no one will swindle you because you will never be trying to get ahead by less than honest methods.

All throughout history, people have been swindled because greed had overtaken them. They failed to see the downside because something for nothing clouded their judgement. Everything has a downside. Everything has a cost. This is true for all things in life. If you devote your energy to one thing, all other things do not get the necessary energy. Many working adults are faced with this today. They work so much that they do not see their kids. It is not always their choice. The lack of balance causes their kids to suffer. So the only choice we have as parents is to do the best with what we have and make the most of the time we are given. This is the essence of life itself. Do the best with what you have and be thankful for it.

I have some final thoughts about money. There are just about as many ways to make money, as there are bills in print. Whatever you end up doing in your life, don't get rich on other peoples' shortcomings. For example, most of America is over-weight and not happy about it. Every month it seems a new solution surfaces and desperate people buy the plan for whatever it sells for, hoping that this product will come through for them. In the end, it doesn't and people get really rich from it. The next month something new comes out and the cycle starts again. The same is true for baldness and get rich quick schemes. All that these things amount to is someone playing on another person's weakness. It is equivalent to a drug dealer who has someone hooked on drugs. Sure, you can make a lot of money, but it is dirty money with a touch of evil. You are taking advantage of those who cannot help themselves and it is not right. Do something where you can be proud to wake up every morning. Try to find something you love to do and get paid enough money to support yourself doing it, whatever it tuns out to be, be able to look yourself in the mirror and smile.

Women. I have left this topic for last, not because I have some fantastic insight on it, but rather more than anything in your life a woman can drive you to substances and make you want to spend all your money on her, like nothing else. Everything has a cost. Finding the right woman and building a lifetime of memories is worth every cent of effort. A word of caution, however, the road that leads up to the woman you marry is often a bumpy, twisted, out of control roller coaster ride of emotion that you can't imagine. It is inevitable. It is a part of life. Think about what's happened and grow from it.

Let me give you two quick semi-related points. If you happen to be gay, that's okay. Just take everything I have written about women and replace it with the word men. The second point is, that out of the three things that give men the hardest time, the loss of a woman is the most painful and may turn your thoughts suicidal. For one reason or another, many people I know have considered taking their own life. It is almost as if it is a prerequisite for living. It is as if when you are at life's lowest point, you start to question if you should you still be breathing. The answer will always be yes. If you get anything from this book, let it be this. NEVER TAKE YOUR OWN LIFE! I have always believed that no matter how bad things got, I could always live my life out alone on a desert island. It is never as bad as you think it is. There are people who have felt the same pain countless times before. Your situation is not unique or original. Learn to grow from it.

11

Getting back to women. I have never really liked lingerie. I have been told that sexy, frilly clothes add mystery and excitement to the woman. I don't get it. To me nothing is more beautiful than the naked body. Why cover it up? I should mention that I do not view pornography as a bad thing, if two criteria are met. #1—No children, children being defined as under age eighteen. #2—Pornography should not be viewed for masturbation purposes.

Now that I am an adult, I do not own any pornography, but it was a must for my curiosity as a boy. How else can a young man see women from all around the world? A word of advice, look at the whole picture. Don't just focus on one part of the body. It is degrading and disrespectful. In most cases you are looking at a beautiful human being. Learn to appreciate the curves and subtle lines that create beauty. Respect that anyone who is posing before you without clothes is proud of whom they are, and you are fortunate that they are willing to show you what they hold special to themselves. The naked body cannot hide flaws, so you are seeing the person's weaknesses as well as strengths. I believe in life that you should practice as close as possible to the real thing. If you view the naked body in photographs as if they are a piece of meat, you will end up treating people the same way. If, however, you grow to have an appreciation for the beauty of the naked body, when the time comes to be naked along side the person you love, you will be that much more in awe at the splendor of their beauty. You will absolutely be humbled by the fact of all the people in the world they could share themselves with, they choose you, and you will be thankful.

I am amazed at the stigmas associated with viewing the naked body. Maybe the day will come when we can knock down the walls and viewing each other will not be perceived as dirty. Another point I have about pornography. If you or your sister, when you are old enough to decide for yourself that you want to pose nude, you have my blessing, but be advised some people in some part of the world will be viewing your photos for the sole purpose of getting their rocks off. Think about it.

There is a crude expression that you are going to hear called "getting your dick wet". It refers to a man rushing to engage in intercourse for the sole purpose of losing his virginity. Sadly, the pressure for men and women to have intercourse at a younger and younger age is increasing. Please learn from my experience. I had intercourse at a young age. I believed I loved the person at the time only to find out I was too young to know what love was.

Looking back I was not ready to become a daddy and I was damn lucky that my irresponsible actions didn't make me one. After two months of a very physical relationship I broke it off with the girl citing a feeling of incompleteness. They say that hindsight is 20/20. Learn from me, not many other fathers will tell you this, but there is absolutely no correlation between having sex and being a man. You are no less a man if you don't rush to have sex. Wait to have intercourse until you find the girl you think you want to spend the rest of your life with. You will thank me later. If the person you are with doesn't respect your decision, then you are with the wrong person. No one who loves you would force you to have sex.

Although it is not common for a man to be forced to have sex in today's age unless he is in prison. The times are changing. On the topic of forced sex, let's flip this around. What is common is that men with severe psychological problems force themselves upon women. The associated word is so commonly used, it has lost its vulgarity. I do not use it. It is a four- letter word that begins with "R". It is vile. If you ever get to know a woman who has been attacked this way, if she can relate the story of her attack to you, you will hear a story that will cause you to be ill. From that point on, if you hear that "R" word, you will retain that ill feeling again.

The part that boggles me is about once a month there is a movie that pertains to this subject and it is generally acceptable. Even more amazing is since shows a need to be original, the writers have to twist the same general plot and make it even more gruesome for shock value. The bad news is that nothing shocks us any more.

A woman can willingly strip her clothes for a camera and that's dirty and wrong, but a woman who has her clothes ripped from her and is sexually assaulted by two boys (Leaving Las-Vegas) wins an Academy Award.

Women are not a piece of meat and should not be treated as such. No one deserves to be forced upon. Males have hormones that must be kept under control. Lust is a powerful thing and any man who thinks that a woman exists to please them is messed up in the head. Believe me, you will know when the situation is presenting itself. It will be a mutual experience. If there is any hesitation on either side, stop immediately before you make a mistake that cannot be undone.

When you do date a woman, try to use the date to form a checklist of what qualities you like and dislike in your future wife. Imagine that any girl you date could someday be your wife. I know it sounds unusual but it adds a certain comfort and respect level to the relationship. Many couples feel an unseen pressure to rush to have sex. Ultimately, it starts their relationship off on the wrong foot and dooms their future from the start. They sometimes don't even get to a second date. Try not to rush. If you feel like there is an unseen rush, slow things down. Love will wait and so can you.

In closing, learn to be patient in every aspect of life. Learn to admit you don't know everything, but listen closely when someone who has been there already wants to teach you. Don't be afraid to ask questions. It's not a sign of weakness. Learn to apologize if you mess up, and even when you don't, thank everyone. No one likes an ungrateful person. It is okay to cry for any reason. Learn to appreciate your emotions. You are the man of the house now. Be strong. I will always love you.

CHAPTER III

TO KEATON

Your chapter is going to be a little harder for me to write than Kieran's. Not being a woman, my opinions are going to be based solely on my observations. I put that warning in only because you may read a line or two and think I am completely off base. I am only going by what I have observed in my life, so be gentle.

We named you Keaton because your mother and I believed it was cool. As a girl, we figured you could use every edge you could get. Anyone who has ever heard your name thought it was cool. Unfortunately, we live in a society where historically women have had a tough time being taken seriously. Although it has gotten better, prejudice against women will always exist. There will always be some men out there that have no interest in your mind or soul, but only view you as a piece of meat. No matter how hard you try to be recognized for your efforts, this individual will secretly be scheming to find some way to coax you into having sex with him. Sadly, it is unavoidable and it is one of the additional unneeded strains of being a female. If you are not overly attractive, no one pays attention to you, and if you are attractive, men will pay attention to you, but there is no guarantee they will be listening to a word you are saying. Chances are they will be nodding their heads like they are listening but secretly they will be trying to picture you naked the whole time. I apologize in advance.

I wrote in Kieran's chapter about things that will cause difficulty in his life—money, women and substances. As a woman, you have these problems plus one or two more that originate from these first three. We will start with substances.

It is my opinion, but I have noticed that women and men drink about the same, but for different reasons. A man will drink for the sole purpose of getting hammered. Men are an abusive group. Drinking itself is a form of abuse. Ask any doctor. The human liver is not happy about alcohol and it does not have an easy time processing it. It is really something your body could do without. A woman will usually drink enough to maintain a high and not really try for that plastered feeling, but sometimes get it any way. If anything, she will underestimate how much alcohol it will actually take to keep the buzz going. Don't get me wrong, some women drink to get slammed as well, but for the most part they only drink socially. The bottom line is abuse is abuse.

Since I have not drank since the age of fifteen, I have had to find another form of abuse for myself. When I get depressed I usually go to a fast-food chain and order three large French fries, dump them into a bag, salt them accordingly, and eat until I get sick. I don't know the psychology of why we self-abuse ourselves but for a few seconds it seems therapeutic. Then I get an ache in my stomach.

Let's discuss smoking. It has been my experience that men usually smoke because they are creatures of habit and only out of pure laziness they won't quit, unless told by a doctor, and even then it's questionable.

A woman is also a creature of habit but is more the type to do things for specific reasons. It has been my observation that most women smoke because there is something wrong in their lives; husbands, boyfriends, money, their job, stress is causing them the need to release through cigarettes. There will always be exceptions to any rule and it was an exception to be the rule that helped me create my theory.

I used to work in a pool hall, the absolute epitome of a smoker's haven. A man came in daily. He used to wear glasses. Some days he smoked, some days he didn't. On the days he would come in and complain of family troubles, his glasses would be yellow from the smoking he did. On the days when his family wasn't driving him crazy, his glasses were clean. It got to the point that I could tell you how things were at his home by the color of his glasses. Clean, life was good. Smokey, was not good. I just got finished telling you men were not like this and here is my exception.

The point that got illustrated to me was that when everything was good in people's lives, they didn't smoke and vice-versa. It became tremendously clear that this held true more for women than men. In fact, I could approach any woman who was smoking, ask her what's wrong in her life, and get a detailed answer. Don't get me wrong. I am not saying people who do not smoke do not have problems, it's just that the people who do smoke, women specifically, smoke less if at all when everything is good in their lives. The desire to smoke should be a red flag that something is wrong in your life.

Consider two other points about women and smoking. It has been proven that women have a harder time quitting once they start. It is very tough for them to stop. There is some kind of chemical that grabs on to women and does not want to let go.

The last point is this. NOTHING makes a beautiful woman less attractive than seeing a cigarette hanging from her mouth. If you ever feel the need to smoke, examine your life. There is probably a stress or a problem that you are going through. Do what you can to remedy the situation without turning to drugs, alcohol or cigarettes. These substances only act as feel good quick fixes and it is no way to live your life. I have always believed that every problem has an answer if you are to be honest with yourself and deal with the reality of the truth. Seek out the truth. Don't hurt yourself in the process. It will only delay your arrival at the truth.

When it comes to money, I feel women have received a bad rap about it. In many households the woman of the house handles the finances. The husband may be bringing the actual check home but it is the wife that gives him an allowance and budgets for the bills, and still manages to save for a rainy day, vacations, etc. This is a feat that most men could not pull off.

There is a term that some women get stigmatized with called a "compulsive shopper". And while it is true that most women I know enjoy to shop, so do most men. We just go about it differently. Everybody enjoys spending money if they have it. It is that men just look at shopping more like a task and women look at is more like therapy. I think that with women, more than not, their spending works more like a stress release and they gain a satisfaction that resembles a job well done.

For example, a woman can be in a mall shopping with friends and come upon a store having a sale on shoes. She didn't come to the mall for anything specific. She just came to see what was there. If you have ever shopped for women's clothes you would know that

Joseph Assante

something new comes in every day and the sizes they have that day, that second, is what they have. No second chances, no reordering tomorrow, nothing in stock. What's there is there and that's it. So many times a woman can justify shopping with the reason she is going to see what's there and have it be a valid reason. So the woman is in the shoe store to see what is there and she finds a pair of shoes for an outfit she purchased three months ago that she hasn't been able to wear because she had no shoes for it. Although she has many outfits at home, and she hasn't seen this one in months, she can tell you in exact detail, down to the button, what this outfit looks like. So she buys the shoes, the outfit is complete, and she feels like more of a whole person because of it.

A man will walk ino the same store, see the first pair of shoes on sale, and without trying them on, buy them. He will bring them home and throw them into his closet where they will set for three years before his wife either throws them out or gives them away to the local charity. Which one seems like the more impulsive story?

The most important thing you need to know about money is to save it, because in life, it never seems like you have enough. At the same time, try not to obsess over it. Many people can't control themselves when it comes to money and then it controls them. Understand that money is the not the most important thing in life. Happiness is. And while the two seem mutually exclusive there are many unhappy rich people in the world who would trade their money in a second for real happiness. Try to be aware about buying things to make your self feel better. It is only a temporary fix. It is okay to reward yourself for your hard work by buying yourself something, just don't do it so often that you become financially strapped and a slave to your credit cards. I have always tried to find happiness in life's simpler things. It is more rewarding. Trust me.

Men. I could easily write that in a nutshell. Ninety-nine percent of men are scum who want nothing more than to have their way with you and will pretend to be your best friend until they do. Then once they have gotten what they wanted, they will toss you aside to pursue their next conquest. As accurate as that may be, ten pages of man bashing would not make for good reading. I want to discuss two semi-related issues that come up with men that give women problems.

18

The first issue is how women end up being abused in a relationship. What I mean by abused is not so much physical abuse, but rather mental abuse. Since I have never majored in psychology, I can't tell you about why a woman stays in a physically abusive relationship. The second a guy hits you, you should be out the door instantly, no second chances. It is an absolute puzzle to me why a woman would put up with that.

The abuse I want to discuss happens every day and girls let this happen more frequently. Here's the situation. A girl falls head over heels for a guy. This scenario usually gets the girl in trouble. They see this guy and falls in love. They know nothing about him except he is beautiful. The girl does everything she can to be noticed by Mr. Dreamboat. The guy usually will respond by doing one of three things…show an interest in her, ignore her, or fake an interest in her to see what he can get out of it, money, sex, whatever.

What the girl fails to realize is that in order for any relationship to work it must start from the same level. It's not something that can be measured like liquid in a jar, but rather you talk about things and see if you share the same interests and likes. As you get to know the person you stockpile things you like and dislike about them. Eventually you have a pretty good idea about what you will put up with in a partner and what you won't. There must be a balance in a relationship. If you don't compare likes and dislikes you may start out with a lopsided relationship whereby you like them a lot and they think you are just okay. What ends up happening is, because your feelings are so strong for that person, you may tend to overlook certain flaws in a person that ordinarily you would not stand for. You may argue with yourself, "Yeah, but he is such a nice guy, except every once in a while he gets drunk and hits me". Normally you would be out the door, but because you're so high in the clouds for this guy, you let that little detail slide and because you are so nuts for him, this person takes advantage of your kindness. I am not saying that this doesn't happen to men as well. Very often a man will go out with a pretty girl without considering the rest of the package and she uses him for all he is worth. The point is that before you go nuts for a guy, consider who he is as a person and know that if you can't come first in his life, maybe he is the wrong person for you.

19

This brings me to my second point. In many cases a woman will find Mr. Right or a man will find Miss Right, and that person will already be married. It goes for both men and women but I know many more women involved with married men than vice-versa. What usually happens is the girl gets promised the world and she hears all about a mythical divorce from the guy she is with that is never going to surface. The problem is, she is afraid to push the guy for fear that she may lose him, when in reality she never had him. Part of "balance" is two people coming from the same place in life. The ages do not have to be the same, just the mindset. Either you are both single or both married and you want out, some kind of scenario where both of you have the same amount to lose by entering into a relationship. Balance means that mentally you are both prepared to enter into a relationship. Not one person looking for commitment versus the other looking for a good time. This is a big problem that both men and women deal with. They enter into a relationship quickly with unrealistic expectations of the outcome.

The only solid advice I can give you about relationships is don't rush. Ninety-nine percent of the time rushing is a bad thing. Of course there will always be exceptions to every rule, but for the most part it is best to wait to get to know each other. Here is a likely scenario. You find a guy who you believe is Mr. Right. One complication is that he is already involved in a relationship with someone else. So what do you do? The answer is wait. Love is tireless. If you care for him now like there is no tomorrow, you can wait for him. The timing is not right and the relationship is doomed right now anyway. The harder you push for it, the more it is guaranteed to fail. In a relationship, there is no greater feeling than equal love; that person caring for you the same way you care about him. Give it some time. What difference will six months make versus the rest of your life, right? The point is, if you start a relationship whereby you are infatuated with that person, it will cause you to look at him with a blind eye. This particular guy may have flaws that you have already spotted slightly, but because you are nuts for him, you are willing to overlook them and for what reason? Your love filled blindness will be used against you, intentionally or not.

This person may be quicker to take advantage of you only because he knows he could get away with it and because he knows that no matter what, you will forgive him. No one is worth compromising your values and beliefs. No one should strive for anything but complete happiness, and having to live your life compromising will not give you happiness completely. If that philosophy sounds a little selfish, understand this. Life is too short to live it unhappily. When you are living unhappily you make everyone around you miserable too. If the people around you really love you, they will be happy when you are. Do what you can to be happy and the people around you will be happy for you.

One more topic that is going to give you stress in life is your looks. In life, people are rarely satisfied with their looks. At some point we all end up looking in front of a mirror naked and make a noise out loud comparable to seeing a large hairy bug.

Part of being happy with yourself, is understanding that you are who you are. Even if, you went up to someone who you thought had the perfect everything, they would probably respond with "no way, my something is too something". There is an expression that says you can't please everyone. Guess what? You are your own toughest critic. Be happy with who you are. Someone will always criticize somebody else. In most cases, those people are taking digs because they themselves have insecurities.

Please do not think you have to look a certain way or weigh a certain amount. Please don't rush to be on a fad diet or get plastic surgery. Try to think past today. If you start a diet, is it something you can continue for the rest of your life? Ask yourself, are you doing what you are doing because in your heart and soul you believe it is the right thing or because your friends are telling you to? Please, do something because you believe in it and be ready to defend your actions to those who would question you.

Sex. I wrote in Kieran's chapter not to rush when it comes to sex and I don't want you to rush either. Please speak to other women about this. Many other women's first times were less than special. Your first time and every time after should be with the man you love and who you believe you would want to marry. It should not be with someone who is pressuring you into it because he wants another notch

21

in his bedpost or someone whose only interest is to convince you he loves you only to sleep with you. Understand this, some men will say whatever he thinks you want to hear to accomplish that goal. A common line you may hear is "If you loved me, you would sleep with me", it is a line older than time itself. Adam probably used it on Eve. There is nothing more sacred than when a woman lays down for a man and spreads open her legs. If the circumstances are right, it will take your partner's breathe away. Please make sure you wait until you feel in your heart it is right. Try not to be trapped or tricked. Once you do it, you can't undo it.

There are two other not so pleasant thoughts regarding sex. If having sex becomes a forced issue, I pray to God it never happens, but it's not always in your control. You do not want to end up alone with a guy you don't know very well in a non-public place. Hopefully, if a situation did develop, you would stay calm and talk your way out of it. Tell him after many, many no's that you would but, you have your period and it's a bloody mess down there, or that you have blisters down there and that you are not sure who you got them from, or stick your fingers down your throat and throw up. Whatever it takes, stay in control of the situation, if you lose your cool...you could lose a part of your soul. I have never been trained on what to do if this happens. I suggest you get trained at a sexual assault center. Talk to other women who have been attacked or sexually assaulted. Formulate a game plan. I hope you will never need it but in the event something goes horribly wrong, you will be prepared for it. Furthermore, if you are more aware that it could happen, you may be able to foresee potentially dangerous situations and avoid them completely.

The second non-pleasant thought is this. No matter what precautions you take every time you have sex, you had better be prepared to become a mommy. The only guarantee is not to have sex at all. Understand that nothing will screw up your life more than having a baby when you are not mentally or physically ready to have one. Some women are never ready, and having a baby doesn't make you any more of a woman and neither does having sex. It doesn't make you more mature to do mature activities. Think about it. Is this the person you want to bring a new life into the world with? What if you are not ready to have a baby? What then? Do you carry the baby to full term and then put it up for adoption? Or do you extinguish its life through abortion? Are these questions you are willing to handle? I am not going to harp on it, but please consider the consequences before the action. In life, everything has a price. It is only a question if you are willing to pay it and if what you are paying for is really worth it.

Some final thoughts I want to leave you with. Be strong. Don't take crap from anyone. Females in general tend to be nice and sweet. Unfortunately, what happens more times than not is that, if you are being sweet, gets mistaken as a weakness that you have. If someone thinks they can take advantage of you, they usually will.

No means no. If you aren't comfortable with a certain situation, don't stay in it. Fight your way out of it if you need to. If you are not happy, fix it, so you are.

Try to be happy alone. Too many times a woman will stay with a man or vice-versa because they can't handle being alone. If you are not happy being alone, how can you be happy with someone else? A relationship is two people bringing their own separate views together and the mesh that happens afterwards. It doesn't work if you have no ideas or opinions of your own of which to contribute to the relationship. You have to realize that you were somebody before whoever came into your life and if they left your life, you would still be that same person, only enriched in some way for knowing that individual. You grow from every relationship and you get a little smarter. The expression goes, "Whatever doesn't kill you makes you stronger".

You are going to spend a large portion of your life keeping men from looking down your shirt and reaching up your skirt. For the most part you will be treated like an object and not listened to for your ideas. Keep your head up. There comes a time later in life when you realize you can have complete control in this male dominated world. A smile, well placed, can go a long way.

Learn patience and gratitude. Nothing is worse than an impatient and ungrateful person. Both of those things have to be learned and it takes time to appreciate things you have versus things you think you want.

Remember you will always be my little girl and if I am not there in your life to see things happen, I will always be in your heart. A day doesn't pass when I don't think about you and Kieran. I love you always.

CHAPTER IV

ABOUT LIFE AND DEATH

I believe in order to have a meaningful discussion about any topic you must look at as many different arguments as possible regarding that topic and take them to their logical conclusion. Based on a theory that a truth is a truth, no matter how it is approached, we can then base an answer to what seems to be an unanswerable question and have it appear pretty sound, leaving the only room for error to be a side of the argument we had not considered. All that being said, I am now going to tackle the big question, what is the meaning of life? And in this chapter, what is the meaning of death as well.

At the young age of seven, I found myself dressing up to go to a wake. For many years to follow, I went to a wake or funeral. Throw into the mix, my dog had to be put asleep. I went to the veterinarian with a dog and I came out with a collar. You can imagine the exposure I had to death at a very early age. It was, however, a good thing because it allowed me to tackle an otherwise unobtainable topic with the clarity of a child.

I asked many questions as a child. Some I had to find my own answers for through interrogating those around me. At my first wake, I asked the big question to as many people as I could corner. "Why do people die?" The response I received was less than rewarding. "It was their time," and "It's God's way," filled the air. Convinced that I asked the wrong question having not received a suitable answer, I reflected. The next year brought the next wake and I struck again, only this time I had a follow up question, "Alright, if you can't tell me why people die, then tell me this. Why do they live?" Silence. It was obvious to me that my questions were not tough, just unanswerable to those people who had not considered the topic. As far as I could tell, no one had even thought to consider it. From that point on it became my mission to figure out the meaning of life.

I developed something. I called it a "childism". A childism is a belief that a child creates about why something is the way it is. These beliefs do not have to be based on any facts, just a child's observations. These beliefs may last a couple of days or weeks or maybe even for the rest of their lives. Something like people who are tall drive red cars, or thunder is really God bowling. Some theory that explains stuff at a level of thought that at the time of creation, the child was thinking at. Later in life, they may modify that theory or give up on it all together.

By the time I was eleven, I came up with my theory about life and it has remained the same since then. My theory on life is this. Life is a circle. It was my observation that in life that things seem to be good, better, great, good, worse, bad, really bad, rock bottom, and then gradually you make you way upwards and the cycle repeats. You may skip some levels of graduation but you end up in the same place. A few years later I modified the theory slightly for some people I observed. Life is a circle inside which there are a series of smaller circles that seem to get bigger as we age. For example, when you are a child it seems during the course of one day you go around at least five circles within one large one. Your life as a whole is great, but you seem to have a series of mini-tragedies. You get a new toy and everything is great. You break it and life is over. You are excited to watch your favorite TV show. You're happy, then you find out it has been moved to a different time slot and your life is over. Such is the life of a child. With adults it's different. We seem to have small victories with the lower parts of the circle, but then when it rains it pours, and then when it is good, all is good except for a few bumps in the road. As adults we can spend long periods of time on the top or bottom of each outside circle. The process may take years, unlike children who make the same trip in hours.

What I was able to do with my theory was give people hope and assurance that things would improve, or let them know that things may actually get worse before getting better, the pain isn't as bad if you expect it to get worse before it gets better.

So, the next question to be tackled was now that I knew how life works, why do we live or die? At the time, I came up with my childism about this. God wasn't really explained in my life so I didn't delve into any explanation with God in the picture. Most people don't think about life or death until they are faced with either one, either through a birth or a recent death, so I kept my explanation brief.

I believe that people exist in your life to affect you. It sounds simplistic, but think about its ramifications. Anyone you come in contact with has a reason or purpose for being there. They exist so you can reach to them one way or another. For example, you may see a homeless person on the street. For whatever reasons, you needed to see that homeless person, either to think about them or maybe you will speak to them later. Whatever the reason, it happened, and their existence has a direct or indirect influence on you. In essence, that person existed because you needed to think about them at some point in your life, either now or later. So I believe that people live to have an effect on others and when they are done affecting the people around them, they cease to exist, figuratively and sometimes literally. Time may pass, and without seeing that person, it is as if they are dead versus they really are dead. In either case, they are no longer around to have an effect on you and in some cases the person's death is more profound than their life, and you might not have a need to think about them until their death. I feel like I am dead to you guys sometimes because we go so long without seeing one another. I am sorry.

Along the same lines there has been much debate over when life begins. I believe life begins when you give that life thought. A book, a stuffed animal, or even an idea could gain life as a result of you thinking about it. The best part is that as long as you give someone or something your thoughts, you keep that person or idea "alive". So if a person close to you does die, you need only think about them from time to time and you will keep their spirit alive, even for just a moment, and you can continue receiving them for as long as you fill your heart and mind with their memory.

Try not to obsess about the whole death thing. Many people get freaked out about death. I am not saying you should go to a local funeral home and jump in a casket. What I am saying is that at some point everyone dies and I think people get bothered by the unknown "are we there yet" factor. At some point in your lives you are going to go somewhere far away. The drive there is going to seemingly take forever. You will be going to an unfamiliar place and you never seem

27

to get there. The anxiety finally gets to you and you burst out with, "are we there yet?" In time, as you go visit that place more frequently, the drive doesn't seem as long and the roads get more familiar. In my mind, this is like the topic of death for many people. They don't like to discuss it or even mention it. So when the time comes in their lives that they have to deal with the topic, their anxieties overtake them and they can't deal with it. Then as time passes and death comes up more in peoples' lives, they become a little more comfortable with the concept. Probably the best advice I can give you so you are not so overtaken by the concept of death is to speak to a person who is terminally ill and who have a positive outlook towards the life they have left. I have spent time with people who are fighting for life "tooth and nail" and they were a wonderful inspiration to me. I thought my life was tough until I sat down with my grandmother. She had many surgeries and many pills she had to consume on a daily basis. I would go to her feeling down on myself for some petty problem and I would see her in a constant state of being uncomfortable and yet with all her discomfort, her motto on life was, "I don't go in the corner for anyone. If you want to drive to Oshkosh, we'll drive to Oshkosh!" She was a tremendous inspiration to me. She helped me feel less sorry for myself. In your lives try to expose yourself to death so it is not such a mystery to you.

Two other points I want to cover about death is murder and suicide. I'll start with murder. I don't think there is a circumstance where I would take matters into my own hands and kill another person, aside from self-defense. If someone is threatening your life or soul, you had better defend yourself by whatever means necessary. If that means someone loses a life, better it be that person, not you. I don't like to hunt or even fish because I don't like the concept of me taking something's life. However, I am a hypocrite because I do enjoy eating meat. I just don't want to be the one doing the killing. I don't understand how one person can take the life of another person. It takes a certain mindset that is beyond my comprehension. I have never been put in that kind of situation and I hope I never am.

As for the other topic, suicide, I feel as if it is almost a prerequisite of life. It seems many people I know have admitted to considering suicide at one point in their life. If you get one main theme from this book, let it be, do not ever take your own life. Suicide is never an answer to anything. I have always believed that no matter how bad life got, I could always run away and live on an island somewhere by myself.

One of the biggest problems suicide creates is the wake of people it affects behind you and all the unanswered questions that surface after your death. With death, people find comfort in being able to point to something as a reason for it. For example, if the person was older, we think that's okay. After all, they lived a long life. If they are sick we blame the disease, and that's okay. If a person commits suicide, even if there is a note, questions still exist. A note is not a guarantee of answers because the written word is open to interpretation. Someone could write a sentence. Two people could read it and get two different meanings from the same sentence. Look at the United States Constitution under the right to bear arms amendment and how many interpretations that has to it.

Not only that, everyone who loves you will blame themselves, even if your note says not to. It is very hard to have someone that is close to you kill them self and not feel responsible for their death. The fact that you had people who loved you and yet, you still chose to kill yourself hurts. I do not know how to steer you away from this enough. Please, please, please don't ever take your own life. You always have options. Things can be worked out. You may feel as if you are at an all time low, but take heart, it will improve. Life is a circle. It is not how high you fall from or how hard you hit the ground, but how long it takes you to get up. Life can't be great all the time. Learn to appreciate the mini victories. Everything you do in life has a price. If you choose one path, you may pass up what was waiting for you down another path, and you never know which choice would have made your life better versus worse. That is what makes life great. In your life, there will be things that you are destined to do. Sometimes fate may provide you with circumstances that make life harder for you to realize your destiny. As an example, I feel that it is destined for me to complete this book for you guys. This is actually my second time writing it. I had a completed version that I was working on rewriting legibly. I wrote the first draft on my lap in the car during traffic and my daily commute, so it was kind of hard to read. In the process of rewriting it, it somehow got "lost" from my locked car. I poured my heart into that book and I am the kind of person that writes until I get it perfect, then I forget what I have written and move on. I could have easily given up, but I believe that things happen for a reason. Maybe there was one sentence I needed to put in that I didn't put in the first time around. Whatever the reason, I will make this version better than the first. You have to learn to flex like a muscle with life's challenges. And like a muscle, the only way a muscle gets stronger is by being torn and rebuilding on itself. Lack of use causes it to shrink and weaken.

Here are some final thoughts about life and death. Learn to keep your head up and understand that life presents you with many situations, good and bad, and they all happen for a reason. Build on your successes and learn from your mistakes. Nothing is so bad that you have to take your own life. There is an expression that says "whatever doesn't kill you, makes you stronger".

Many people do not know this about me, I write a lot of poems. I even have written a few greeting cards. I love poetry and for whatever the reason, the words seem to flow nicely from my head and I can usually write something good within a few minutes. When Debbie's grandfather passed away, I was moved by how it affected her. She had not had a lot of experience with death, so I wrote her this poem. She liked it so much she showed it to everyone at the wake and funeral in hopes that it would inspire others, here it is…

A Moment

Every six seconds a new life is born,
And every eight someone lay down to die.
Some deaths are senseless and without meaning,
And others, we completely understand why.

It's a persons' job in life to affect others,
And leave a memory in their heart.
Some relationships get to last a lifetime,
And others barely get to start.

It doesn't matter how things were left,
When we pass to the place unknown.
Peace seems to be found for those who deserve it,
And for those with a pure heart, the whole truth gets shown.

So do not mourn for the one you have lost,
Death is an unavoidable endeavor.
Keep a moment with that person in your mind that made you once smile,
And you will keep them alive forever!!

The next chapter talks about people, perception and non-science. Some people go through life completely asleep and do not notice the world around them. Hopefully the next chapter will help you to understand life and the people in your life a little better. It will help you to understand where people come from, give you some perspective, and help you understand why the world is like it is.

CHAPTER V

ABOUT PEOPLE, PERCEPTION AND THINGS NON-SCIENCE

In the last chapter we discussed how good or bad, everything happens for a reason. The secret to living a relatively happy life is understanding where you are on the circle of life and accepting that good and bad things happen and understanding where it fits and relates to your learning process. Some lessons take longer to learn than others and some lessons never get learned.

People are generally ungrateful. As time moves forward, we have become a society that has replaced thank you with what took you so long? Of course, there are always exceptions to most rules and for the most part, I am generalizing, but try to do your part to be more grateful. The problem with not having gratitude is this. Without gratitude, people cannot be thankful for what they have. If they do not appreciate what they have, they will always want more and more. If they always want more and more, they will never be satisfied with what they have now. Consequently, they can never be happy. This is a problem that plagues society today. Nobody is content with what they have. Nothing is enough. Again, there are exceptions to every rule and I hope you two are two of them.

People, for the most part, enjoy routine and will fight you from changing their routine even if they are not happy with their lousy one. It has been said that we are creatures of habit, meaning once we form something into a habit we will do it well, just don't ask us to change it.

People over celebrate holidays and under appreciate the other days. This is a part of the first two generalizations at work. We work and work and unless fun is scheduled via birthdays and holidays, we do not take time to unwind. Then when we do, we do not appreciate the time away from work enough, nor do we appreciate our time spent with family and it gets viewed more as a chore than something pleasant.

People do not feel comfortable talking about death or sex, but they have no problem watching either one on television. These two topics probably affect people most and yet no one can comfortably discuss it. I am amazed at how many married couples do not talk about death or sex. I have always felt there should not be any topic that cannot be discussed openly. We are all people. We all feel the effects of the same things, so why can't we discuss them? People do not think about life until it is threatened, or love, until it is lost. Just as everyday you should treat a loved one like every day is their birthday, there shouldn't be a topic that can't be discussed every day as well.

Once a person becomes a parent it is like a little switch goes on inside them and they now have a parental instinct that can be transferred to anyone else's child. All color boundaries get dropped. All religious boundaries get tossed aside. Whatever reason you could name for two people not getting along gets flushed when it comes to looking out for the welfare of a child. We all look out for one another. Regardless of who we are as people, our kids bind us. We all have the same goals.

I feel that people really have no problems co-existing with others until they begin to seek out their own identity. At that point everything becomes a competitive "mine is bigger than yours" contest where the rules get flushed and we no longer treat our fellow human beings with any kindness. It suddenly becomes all about me. You go from being a sweet little kid who plays nice with everyone to a prima donna who won't play with so and so because they don't look like you or shop at the same stores. Or maybe you won't play with them because they are shorter than you or fatter than you. Whatever the reason, I believe it all starts with that quest for individualism.

As I was going through the ranks at school, I began to notice a pattern, of what kids got picked on and by whom. I formed a childism about people in general. I concluded that people fall into two categories, good or bad. If they were good people, I did everything I could to make their lives easier. If they were bad, I tried to make their lives tough, especially if they made the good peoples lives tough. Unfortunately, I was sometimes portrayed as a bully. I was always trying to do the right thing. I have always had an image of myself that I was a hero to somebody. Everybody needs a hero. I have always wanted that someone to be me. The heroes always helped those in need and I have always strived to help others, kind of a Robin Hood without the money.

About the same time I was working on my life is a circle theory, I was also working on a childism that could define human behavior and explain why people behave the way they do and predict their behavior. I called it the Pendulum Theory.

I believe that morality fixes us at a point. From that point our behavior can then swing us from side to side. One side being good and the other side is bad. The catch is that our judgment puts the pendulum in motion, one way or the other. I believe that, like a pendulum, people whose behavior swings in one direction can only swing back in an equal direction. Or to rephrase it, people who have a capacity to be good to a point have an equal capacity to be bad. Consequently, a person who goes through life never really committing good acts probably will never kill anyone. There has to be a relationship where you have to know one to know the other. It doesn't matter if you ever exercise these capacities. It is merely a question of you have it or you don't. I actually started writing a movie I called, "When The Pendulum Swings", about this very topic. I haven't finished it yet but it will be my next effort.

Let's talk about how people treat each other. I have always believed that when you judge people, you should judge them on their actions, not their words. Ideally, you should not judge anyone, but it is not realistic to think we don't. Everyone does, at least I am honest enough to admit it. Having dealt with people on a retail basis and in my own personal life, you come to realize that most people are good people trying to hustle like the next guy and make a better life for themselves. When people get hung up on a person's background, (color, nationality, etc.), you tend to cloud up the water and not give that person a chance to be seen for who they really are. I always try to give people a chance until they give me a reason not to. Since we already know that people exist pretty much for us to be affected by them, let's talk about that.

This falls under the realm of perspective. Put simply, how a person views things. Everything we read, speak, hear, you name it, is affected by our individual perspective, but I believe all that input is interpreted by what we need as input at that time in our lives. For example, I may look at a picture and tell you the person in the picture is sad. Another person may look at the same picture and say the person is happy. I may need to see a sad person today but tomorrow if I look at the same picture I may need to see a happy person, so tomorrow I may think the person in the picture is happy. The ink-blot tests are classic for this. The examiner, opens up an ink- blot, and asks, "tell me what you see?" You can imagine how many different things he hears. In English class, the teacher will ask the class to read a certain piece of literature. She then will ask the class what the author meant when he wrote a certain line. It is amazing the different answers she would get and everyone was reading the same words. I once read a book by Richard Bach called "Illusions". The story had a character opening up a magic book that had no writing on the pages. Only in times of need, could he open it up and find advice that would get him through his time of need. Many times I have spoken to people and I know the words that left my mouth is not what they heard. It is as if they heard what they wanted to hear. I have watched movies and then watched the same movies again ten years later and got completely different interpretations of the same film. The movie had not changed but, at that point in my life, the perspective I viewed life in had. The point to all this, is that it's been my observation that everything in life happens for a reason and you need only sit back and pay attention to the details as they come up. It is something you have to stop and think to ask yourself, why would this be this happening around me? Certain things will seem to fall into place too easily. You find yourself looking at thirty-eight cents on your dresser and not knowing why at the time. Later that day you are buying something at the store only to be short the same thirty-eight cents. Now you knew why you were looking at it. You were supposed to take it with you. The more you pay attention to little details like that, the more things will reveal themselves to you about your life. It is hard to explain. Pay attention is all I can tell you.

Perspective goes both ways. It is not only about how we view things, but how you are viewed as well. A classic example of this is when you go to school with a new haircut. You feel almost naked. It is your first day out with your new haircut and you are very uncomfortable with how it looks. Your world is over. You want to try every possible move not to be seen. I used to be so embarrassed. Either my dad or my sister cut my hair and as my school photographs can attest, it didn't go so good. It is either that classic situation, or the one where you go to school with a huge pimple on your face. I used to look in the mirror and picture this pimple on my face was going to declare statehood. In both scenarios, I wanted to hide. I went to school afraid and embarrassed of whatever my affliction was that day, and I got abused and picked on. Everyone noticed. As time went on I realized the less I paid attention to my problem that day, the less anyone else did either. I found out that if I ignored my problem and went about my life, no one noticed my pains as if they were invisible. It is also a talent you are going to have to practice. It's all about having confidence and having the ability to project that confidence. It is a talent that can get you places in this world. My problem is that on interviews I would project too much and people would be afraid to hire me because they thought if they did, I would take their jobs. Or I would appear cocky. Nobody likes cocky. Everyone has flaws. Over-confidence is one of mine. The bottom line about this is that you will find out that many things aren't as bad as they seem and if you stick some things out you will find out you went through them to learn a lesson.

There is an old advertising expression that says there is no such thing as an original idea. Every idea is a spin-off from some other basic idea. Along the same lines, there is no such thing as an original dilemma. No situation or problem that you encounter will be unique. So as bad as things seem they are, it is okay. Other people have been in the same jam and lived to tell about it. Nothing is that bad, no matter how you perceive it to be. If you realize, that everything happens for a reason and that one of those bigger reasons is that you are going to have to learn from it, you will be OK. Depending on how good your perception is will determine how much you learn. It is a talent that you must develop. If something drops in front of you, look out for someone to slip on it. Practice, it will come to you.

In the second part of this chapter we talk about "things non-science". Simply put, life is going to throw you things that challenge your perceptions and your thought processes. These things will fall into the realm of things non-science or things not based on any real facts, but that you perceive as real. In life, you are going to come across certain things that can't be defined or understood, as we know it right now. In ten years, we may know every answer to every question for now we cannot cure the common cold.

For ages, people have done "magic" tricks that appear unexplained. As time went on, certain information became common knowledge and these people needed to come up with new ways to make people believe in magic.

As time goes on, you guys will encounter all new things that claim the unbelievable. Be careful. Question everything. Chances are, if your first instinct says it can't be, you are probably right. I am going to give you a few opinions on some general non-science things you will probably encounter. Is there alien life on other planets? Are there really UFO's? I do believe in life on other planets and UFO's, although I doubt we will ever know about them. The government, who watches all things, in all places, would probably know about it first and make sure no one else knew about it. Life on other planets rates right up there with the second coming of Christ, panic wise. Add to the mix that I have yet to see the government handle any program that actually works, so I highly doubt the little green guys would stand a chance.

As for magic or witchcraft, I do not know enough about either. I know magic is more illusion than anything else and the whole "secret" is making the audience believe. I have seen some pretty amazing stuff in my life and what I believe is that I cannot explain it. The latest magician I have seen that is absolutely outstanding is David Blaine. He does a trick where he floats off his feet! He is really great. As for witchcraft and spells, I refer to your Uncle Tony, your Godfather. He knows everything you would need to know about witchcraft. He is the guy to ask. I do believe in things that cannot be explained by science but only because I do not think we can explain them yet because we do not know enough about us. Probably the most significant case in point is ESP, the ability to read minds. I believe that people can read other peoples' minds so long as they are receiving other peoples' thoughts at the right frequency. I believe that people think right now, at a frequency that science cannot measure and being able to focus in on their thoughts is no different than tuning in a radio station so long as you find the right frequency. A perfect example is mother's intuition or sixth sense. For whatever reason, through birth or bonding, a mom can tell if their child is screwing up somewhere or in danger. I believe they are thinking on the same frequency. It is already a natural phenomenon that women who become roommates within a few months have their menstrual cycles adjust, until they all have it at the same time. It is wrong to think that our thought frequencies wouldn't do the same. I will give you two more examples. How many couples do you know that finish each other's sentences? Do you know how many inventors almost didn't get the credit for their ideas because, at the same time they were racing to get their idea patented, somewhere else in the world someone else was trying to make good on the same idea. It has been said that minds think alike, maybe a mind works like a radio, it is able to receive like signals and receive like tuning in your favorite radio station? Maybe ESP is nothing more than being able to receive everyone's signal and a person with the right ability need only turn down the dial to receive everyone's signals, and just like a radio, certain things cause reception to be unclear. Maybe if we could boost our signals or remove any static interference we all could read minds. It is a thought and now that it has been thought, maybe someone with a like mind can make it happen.

I believe the 1990's should be known as the decade of the psychic. Never before in history has there been such a push for psychics. The 1-900 dial-a-psychic hotline thing couldn't spread fast enough. It seems everyone wants some kind of insight on life, and doing the psychic thing has become a new religion. Only now there is a really big push to talk to the spirits of the dead. Psychics are now surfacing who don't predict the future, but make contact with those who have passed away. They "communicate" with those who have passed and answer questions that you didn't get to ask the person when they were alive.

Hands down, the greatest guy I have ever seen is a man by the name of John Edward. He refers to himself as a "radio psychic" and now has a TV show where daily he helps people from here communicate with people who have passed away or as he puts it, "crossed over". He is amazing. I have heard him many times speak to person after person and tell them things from people who have passed away that only each other could know. He told a lady about when she was six years old in a bus station with her father, and they had saw something strange written and joked about it. It was a story that only the two of them knew. I have no idea how he does it.

The problem is, you would have to believe in life after death or some fashion to believe in this. That doesn't exactly jive with main - stream thinking about what happens when we die. That would mean there is a whole world we don't know about full of dead souls. This is not in line with the whole Heaven thing, that's OK. I have an open mind and I think anything is possible. When I was a boy, I used to have many strange dreams. I found that if woke up suddenly, then fell back asleep, I would have strange dreams. It got so interesting that I bought a second alarm clock and would intentionally wake myself up a few minutes before I really had to get up. The few seconds I was awake to shut off the first alarm clock was enough time to make me fall into a surreal world of dreaming. What I found was during the day while I was awake I would experience a flashback of a memory of when I was much younger on the mornings I did this. I would have dreams about getting hurt and when I woke up whatever got hurt in the dream, would hurt me at that time. It got pretty weird. I stopped because it was giving me headaches during the day. I would love to sit down with some dream researcher and attempt to do it again under controlled conditions. They say the brain only works at a small capacity of its true capability. I used to feel like I was in a different world when I did that. I used to wake up exhausted as if I had been up all night. I wonder if I was using some untapped portion of my brain?

How many people do you know that appear to live in different worlds? They don't seem to be able to function in the real world. I am not fond of sports at all. I purposely try to avoid them, and yet there are people I know who aren't athletic at all, yet absolutely live for sports. Their whole world is sports. They can barely function without working sports into the picture. Geniuses are said to live in their own world. Einstein had seven days worth of the same outfit because he couldn't function in our world and yet his ideas were out of this world. There are people with trance-like diseases that have their body here and what appears like their mind elsewhere, or how about this crazy one? When you are asleep your body stays here and your essence goes off and does functions in another world. That is why sometimes you wake up more tired than when you went to bed and you have memories of a dream that seemed way too real. Maybe the other world's concept isn't so inconceivable. Maybe this is what thinking about things non-science is all about. Learn to open your mind, use your imaginations. Going to the moon seemed far-fetched in the 1950's and yet commonplace in the 1990's.

How about ghosts? Are there people dead in spirit form floating around us? There are many, many people who claim to have seen a ghost. They swear their house is haunted and that they live with ghosts. I have never seen a ghost so I couldn't tell either way. I refer again to your Uncle Tony, your Godfather. He has studied about things non-science more than anyone I know and I consider him an expert. If you ask him a question about a topic he doesn't know anything about, he will find out for you.

A better question should be, what happens when we die? Do we go to heaven or hell or limbo or nowhere? Do such places exist or is it merely a figment of imagination? If you believe in God, you believe in heaven. Some cultures believe you die and your soul gets reincarnated. You could die today and come back tomorrow as a dog or fish. I have a slight problem with that but I must say I have seen some pretty smart dogs, but I doubt there is a correlation. Reincarnation seems believable to me, as strange as the concept sounds, because when I look at children four years old and playing Beethoven on the piano, you have to wonder how that is possible. Is it that they have a greater capacity to learn or is it that they are retaining information from a past life? In general, you have to question some peoples' ability to learn something more easily than the next person. Other people spend a lifetime trying to do things without ever learning them. Maybe we already have a lifetime of knowledge already waiting for us inside our head. All we have to do is remember it. Did you ever notice some people are absolute naturals at certain things? It is as if they spent a lifetime doing something and they are just remembering how they did it last time around versus actually learning it for the first time. How else do you explain a person who cannot do logical math, but can take apart an engine piece by piece and rebuild it. What about a child prodigy who can tell you about quantum physics but cannot tie his own shoe? It's something to consider.

Some final thoughts about these topics are these. Have an open mind. There is an expression. The mind is like a parachute. It doesn't work unless it's open. I believe that any idea that can be thought could probably happen in reality. Anything is possible.

There is another expression that says, "You are what you believe you are. If you believe what you think, what you think will become a reality." Put another way, if you believe in your heart something can be a reality, one day it may be. If what I have written in this section seems too unreal that is okay. I put this section here to prompt your imagination and get your creative juices flowing. You are the future of tomorrow the ideas you create today may help people tomorrow. Believe and it will happen for you.

Life is more than what you find on TV or in a computer. We are quickly becoming people that rush to do things thought up for us, not people who think for themselves. We do things and don't consider why we are doing them. We tend to judge others and not ourselves. We go about our days working, for the weeks end and rushing to retire rather than absorbing in every day and every detail. Most of what we believe is just someone else's opinion that we have adopted as our own. Rarely do we think something out ourselves. We usually take someone else's opinion and jump on the bandwagon with it.

Most of this chapter talks about topics that people are afraid to discuss without looking silly or stupid.

I am terrified that you guys are going to grow up with your best friend being a computer or having a friend that only can discuss current events and not delve into the meaning of life and the events within it. There is more to life than the Internet. My generation grew up on TV. Yours is going to grow up "on line". I used to stay up late watching TV. You guys will be losing sleep in a chat room somewhere. With TV anything you saw, you took with a grain of salt. With the Internet, it often gets forgotten that anything you see may not be true. A computer seems like a more reliable source when in reality it is less reliable because anyone can hack anything on to it and have it pass for fact. The bottom line is this. Have an open mind and don't be afraid to question anything in life that doesn't seem right and don't accept anything that seems right as law. I love you guys.

CHAPTER VI

ABOUT MARKETING AND GOD

There are many people in the world who would rather take your money and who could care less about your happiness. On a daily basis, everyone is trying to get you to buy something through some form of marketing. Some approaches are more casual but it is all about the money. We always have advertising around us, even if you don't realize it. In most cases the people who want your money would prefer you not think about your actual purchase but rather have you just hand over your money. To help distract you, they will use one of two diversionary tactics. They will use words you don't understand to make it sound like it is the cure for whatever ails you, or they will use sex.

This method has boomed off the map in the 1990's. Sex sells everything today. Part of the problem is that in this society everyone wants to have sex, but no one wants to talk about sex or at least not casually with the opposite sex. The more it is not talked about the more taboo the topic becomes and the higher the shock value when it is glaring at us on the TV screen or magazine. The more it will sell when see it.

Lack of discussion about sex is actually a huge problem in this country. More diseases get spread, more unwanted pregnancies happen and more marriages break up from all this non-discussion.

It is amazing what a man will buy if you put a half-naked woman next to it. Most of the men in the world in general would buy any product if a pretty woman were put in front of it. Either that or make it somehow related to sports. If you combine both elements, for example, professional wrestling, you get the most popular thing in sports entertainment. I am actually stunned at how much of most men's lives get wasted watching sports. Men don't just watch sports they consume it like a meal. They can tell you every player, their background, current statistics, mother's maiden name, everything you can imagine. To me it is an amazing waste of time and energy. Let's say the average man spends eight hours a weekend watching sports. Imagine that we tape these shows instead of watching them live. If we fast forward through the commercials we would save about two hours of viewing time. Now imagine that we use those two hours for some kind of good use instead of wasting it. Time with the kids or his wife, how many marriages would be saved? I am not saying men should not have time to unwind and relax. Many women enjoy kicking back and enjoy watching sports as well. Too much of anything is no good and men in general are not good at moderation. We overdo.

One of the biggest things that people don't consider when it comes to their distractions is this. It is okay to have distractions to help release stress from daily life. The problem arises when that same daily distraction takes away from your ability to complete your goals. It doesn't take much for your distraction to become an obsession. Only you don't realize it's got you. Let's take cigarettes for example. For whatever reason you started, maybe in your mind you believed they would relax you. You started smoking a few each day only during stressful times and now it has blossomed into two packs a day. The cigarettes own you now. Every free moment you get is spent smoking and since you really need to smoke a ton, you are "making" free moments that are affecting your job and your livelihood. This habit owns you. Pleasure is okay so long as it doesn't own you and it is up to you to be honest about this. Marketing people will tell you both can co-exist and that you can indulge all you want without repercussion. The primary reason I wrote to you guys about this topic is because I want you to recognize that in every stage of your lives you are going to be bombarded by some form of marketing attempting to influence how you define your life. They will tell you that you are overweight as society sees it and try to sell you a diet pill. They will dictate that being bald is wrong and a bald pill will fix it. Don't let these people challenge who you are. Be proud of who and what you are. Marketing's goal is to sell a product to you, not fulfill or satisfy any real need only to fabricate one and go from there.

I want you to understand how powerful advertising is and its affect on how you think and live. It is subtle many times and you don't realize it until its too late. Positive attitude is everything. Let's say life is bumming you out, which it often does. You see a product on TV guaranteeing to un-burn you out. You get a one- month supply of "Product X" for only $19.95. They don't tell you what's in it, but three sexy women and one hunk explain how it changed their lives, so you order it. You don't care what's in it. You just know that they claim it will make you feel great. So you take "X" and within a short time you feel great. You can't imagine life without it so you call the company to order more only to find out that it is available at store "Z" for a little more money. You go down to the store and find it on the shelf for $39.99 a bottle, but you don't care. You get them home and take them only to find these "X" don't give you the "kick" of the old "X", so you have to take more than usual. The problem is now you are running out fast, so you run down to store "Z" and find out they are now $59.99 a bottle while supplies last. The company is going to base their headquarters in Europe, so this may be the last of it. You buy up the last four bottles only to find now instead of five pills each day you are up to one or two every hour. What are you going to do? You are desperate. It still makes you feel great but soon it will be gone. You call the company directly and they tell you they will give you an unlimited supply for only $199.99 a year. Just send the money to the Europe headquarters and you will be a lifetime member. The sucker you are now, you send the money with glee. After all, you really can't live without the stuff now anyway. Weeks pass. The phone number to company "X" has been disconnected. Store "Z" now denies ever selling "X" and it appears "X" as a whole has vanished into thin air. You have a constant headache and you just heard on the news the "X" company is being sought after by the government for selling sugar and caffeine pills because so far three people have died, two diabetics and a man with a weak heart.

What have you learned? If you are like most people, nothing. In fact, after a year or so, the "Y" company will surface selling this new and improved product that is guaranteed to make you feel great, only this time around they will use three hunks and a half-naked girl and the cycle will start all over again.

People, for the most part, are never fully satisfied with what they have. They have no gratitude for what they have and, therefore, do not appreciate what they have. If you can't be happy with what you have, you will always seek more things that you think will make you happy. Not realizing that your biggest flaw will keep the vicious circle going forever, you will never have happiness completely. Please don't fall for this trap. Marketing people know this and live for it. They have to make your present life appear inadequate. If you were happy, you wouldn't need to buy anything from them. Get it?

I have some final thoughts about marketing and advertising and its effect on your lives. "Caveat Emptor" means buyer beware in Latin. Even ancient Rome had its share of con men trying to separate people from their money. In my Dad's time the marketing people made you feel like you had to own the perfect car and that you weren't a man if you didn't smoke or drink a certain brand of product. In my time, you are nothing unless you are physically fit without wrinkles and a full head of hair. You absolutely must have the fastest computer, a luxury car, and the best brand name everything from the local electronics chain.

In your time, it's hard to say but history dictates the bar doesn't get lower. The next logical attack is genetics. You will probably be told that you have flawed genes, and that for only $299.00, you could be injected with a gene boosting enhancer that will have you thinking like Einstein, drawing like Pablo Picaso, playing music like Mozart and giving you a body that is genetically sound that will last one hundred and fifty years. They will show you the closest thing to a Greek God and Goddess and say they owe it all to that product.

Please be careful and suspicious of anything free, get rich quick, lose weight fast or anything else that sounds too good to be true or too much like a product is playing God. On that note, let's discuss the second part of this chapter, God.

At some point in your lives you are going to be confronted with the issue of God. In my life I was sent to church in my early years in hopes that the church would positively influence me. However, I did not spend my time listening to the priest, but rather scanning the church for cute girls. Later in life I attended CCD classes which also proved an excellent location for spotting girls if I made it that long because I frequently got sent home for being bad.

Interestingly enough, at my confirmation the priest read a long passage from which we were supposed to take some sentences from and incorporate into our lives, and just as I managed to get eye contact with a girl, I could feel the priests' eyes on me. I quickly looked him in the eye "and he became man". He said the passage was over and that line was what I took from it. From that point until now, every misstep I have taken, every good thing gone unappreciated by me, every time that black cloud my uncle once told me followed my actions, would surface to cause my world to crash around me. The voice of that priest echoes in my head, "and he became man".

It was as if all the good things I did piled up on one side and all the bad things on the other side and it was a question of which foundation I was going to place my pedestal to stand on into manhood. The unfortunate news is that in my life I had placed little rocks on the side of good and boulders on the side of bad. No matter how high I built the foundation of bad, it always seemed easier to climb it.

Now about two years after my metamorphosis I stand on a pile of pebbles constantly fighting to stay on top, eclipsed in the shadow of the mountain of evil I spent most of my life building. At a point in my life I stole something every day. I thought I was Mr. Smart Guy. I shop lifted from every store I went into. I romanticized it in my brain that I was like James Bond. No security system could catch me. I also fantasized I was like Robin Hood because if I stole something I couldn't use, I made no attempt to sell it. I would give it away. In my little mind it was a sort of washing away the sin. I figured I made someone's life better by me stealing so it was a good thing.

I stole money from friends, family and strangers. Which is ironic because I have already told you I have never had a love for money. Either I had it or I didn't. Many a summer's day I spent dumping quarters into video games and buying kids I went out with food. The more I stole, the better time we all had.

I lived by my own rules, laws and codes of honor, the perfect recipe for disaster. Sooner or later it was all to come to a head. It was in September of 1998. I had been working about 70 to 80 hours a week in a local diner. Keaton was due to be born in October and I was in financial trouble. Business had been slow and I was way behind on bills. I knew that I would have to take at least a week off from work to help the birth recovery process and take care of Kieran who was only about eighteen months old at the time.

I have always had a backup plan in my head that I hoped I would never have to resort to. I was going to rob a bank. I was twelve years old when I first began casing this bank to rob it. I used to sit outside it and practice timing the robbery. My escape vehicle changed over the years, from my bicycle to a moped and eventually a car. I had modified and fine- tuned my plan for eighteen years and now I was ready to carry it out.

There was a problem, however. There is an expression that says, "A person is only as strong as their weakest link". My weakest link was my ability to be recognized. I could have dressed in a full monkey suit with colored contacts in my eyes and I would still get nailed for sure. No matter what, I didn't feel I could conceal my identity.

It was 2:30 early Saturday morning. The place was empty. I was in the kitchen leaning up against the bread warmer staring at the ceiling. I had just made up my mind that I was going to rob my favorite bank and the only image I could perceive was myself sitting in a prison cell, the future that would surely come to pass if I did indeed rob the bank. The thought of not seeing the kids again, raced through my head. I would have missed Keaton's birth and my boy growing up to be a man. I started to cry. I started thinking to myself that I desperately wanted a choice. How do honest people get by, I thought? Why was life putting me in such a predicament? The answer to my rhetorical question rang loud and clear. I was the problem.

I had been playing God long enough and failing miserably. The truth was, life was bigger than my little brain could handle. I was about to bring down my life completely. I needed help. Tears were streaming down my face. I looked up into the corner of the kitchen and began to pray. "Please, God, help me. I know I haven't lived a life you could be proud of but until now no one has really been hurt except me. I know I am destined to fail at the bank robbery, but things seem hopeless and the thought of a prison cell isn't going to help the kids. I stand humble before you. I am tired of being the bad guy and I want to start being a good guy. I don't want to be a criminal. I want to fix things. I need help. Please help me. Amen.

My usual routine on Saturday mornings was to food shop. I got off work at 5:00 A.M. and made it home by 6:35 A.M. Your mom was up and she told me to call her dad, my old painting boss. I had worked with him since I was fifteen years old. The economy was horrible when I graduated from college. I had received a degree in Marketing, but when the economy is bad, the first thing companies cut out of the budget is Advertising. So I stepped into painting. I stopped working for him when Kieran was born. Because he ran into tough times he couldn't afford to keep me as an employee. I thought for sure the painting company was going to go under, but it didn't, and his big news was that he had just received an unbelievable amount out of nowhere and he wanted to know if I would come back to work with him. Within two weeks, I was back on my feet financially. It was a miracle! I asked and received a bona fide miracle. Now it was my turn to live up to my part of the deal. Back when I was praying, faster than I could speak the words, I had made an agreement in my thoughts. Grant me this miracle and I will stop my thieving ways. Help me to choose an honest life and I will do my best to uphold my end of it. I immediately began trying to live a "clean" life, a tall order for me. It has been an amazing on-going struggle.

My next step to living clean was to fix some of my previous lies. I felt the thing to do was to tell all the people I wronged what I did and that I was sorry and hope they forgave me. I had been a lousy creep and the only reason I could think I needed to do this was because I needed to complete my end of the bargain. I had never gone to confession. I didn't really believe in it. I have never understood the process whereby you tell a priest all your sins. In CCD class they used to force us to do it. It had always seemed like a great waste of time to me. After all, God is all knowing. Why would I need a third party to mediate for my sins? I could not believe if my prayers are sincere and genuine I would be turned down. So rather than sit with a priest for a day or two I decided to go right to the source. I had committed many crimes against my mom and dad so I sat them down first. Over the course of an hour I retold the diner story and then began telling of the volumes of crimes I could remember. They were stunned. I'm sure they knew I was bad, but not that bad. My parents were disappointed but they understood. They are the most loving and compassionate people I know. My biggest regret with them is the time in my life when I pushed them away. I thank God everyday for them and people like them in my life that were kind enough to forgive me.

Since the diner I have done what I could to live life on the right side of the law and so far I have been doing well, but I would not exactly call myself perfect yet. So far I am a guy who believes in God. It is a good first step after a lifetime of believing in nothing. I do not attend church but every Sunday I try to listen to a radio minister by the name of Ravi Zachiarias. He is smart, witty and well rounded. So when I can, he is my church and my inspiration.

Believe it or not, I once considered being a priest but I couldn't get past the abstinence thing. I believe that if God went back to Adam after the whole apple incident and told him everything would be restored the way things were if Adam would abstain from sex with Eve, Adam's response would be don't change a thing. It's not that I worship sex, but not having it can't be healthy.

I have some final thoughts about God. In the back of every atheists mind is the realization that they could be wrong. I had always believed that when I thought the way I did it would have been because God made me that way. So I covered my bets both ways. I was wrong and that falls under the category of free will, but again, I was Mr. Know-it-all about everything. I had you baptized because I didn't want to screw you guys later in life. If I was wrong I wasn't going to take you down with me.

People used to ask me if I believed in God and my standard answer was, "No, not at this time in my life", mainly because if you tell people you are an atheist, they look at you like a freak. Also I assumed that if God did exist he would find a way to show me. And the believer in God would tell me, "What about your two healthy kids, wasn't that a miracle from God?" The answer should be yes, but if you are a bitter, ungrateful person you tend not to appreciate what is given to you and chalk up what was a complete blessing to luck.

One side of me wishes you could grow up having your own choice about religion and the other side of me wants you to learn from my mistakes and believe right now. I don't feel it is an issue that should be pushed on a person. They must decide in their heart on their own. All I can do is tell you how it went down for me. As Santa Clausian as it sounds, I do believe in God. I have heard that such a belief is weak minded. I contend that believing in God is no more weak minded than joining the military, or going to work for a large company, or walking towards someone you love when they hold out their hand and says, "come, walk with me".

CHAPTER VII

ABOUT MOM

Your mom did not like me when she first met me. In fact, for the first month she tolerated me at best. She was seventeen and drove a red Firebird and I was fifteen and sported a red BMX bicycle. I had a Moped for a short time, but I didn't like driving it to see her because the helmet would mess my hair. I was one hundred percent ego and cockiness. If attitude had a poster boy, I was it. She was a senior in high school and I was a sophomore. At that point in my life… a huge disparity. The first time we actually had contact was your mom walking in on me and another girl at a party fooling around. Not exactly a great first impression. After a few weeks of catching glances of her I had a situation present itself where I could really meet her. She and my cousin Linda played softball together so she would drive Linda home, which coincidentally is two houses away from mine. So one day I "accidentally" missed the bus. I made it a point to bump into Linda. Being the kind person she was, she suggested I get a ride with her. I did and I found myself in the back of your mom's car. It was a short ride and she caught me staring at her several times. Until now, I had never really looked at her. I couldn't help myself. I'm the kind of person that will get caught looking at a person every time. Because once I start the looking, I don't stop. I look deep into a person. It is not that I do a head to toe check out. That's rude. I look at them when they are focused on something else and sneak into the back of their head. I try to imagine what kind of life they have had. I picture them when they were younger and picture ahead to what they will look like when older. It is a little game I used to play when I was younger. When we got to Linda's house I thanked her and walked the rest of the way home. After all, tomorrow was another day and I was patient.

The next day brought the next ride home and this time I didn't rush home. I hung back to get to know your mom better. I remember seeing "that look" in Linda's eyes. I had made quite a habit of getting close to her girlfriends. I grew up with a crush on Linda and since I couldn't date her, I did the next best thing and tried to date her friends. I talked to your mom for about fifteen minutes. Day by day our talks got better. Before long, she would be bringing me up to my house whether or not Linda was even around. It was a strange time for me. I never had a girlfriend who could drive me anywhere. So it became instant freedom for me. Any time I didn't want to be around my parents, all I had to do was make a call and I was gone.

Our relationship had its ups and downs. Your mom broke up with me four times. One time lasted nine months and she was proposed to by another man. I had to sit back and watch and be patient and hope that it wouldn't work out. Your mom wanted her space to figure out what she wanted in life. When that happens there is no way to force a result. If it is meant to be, it is meant to be, and that is the way it is. I was patient. I knew that because we weren't together now didn't mean we wouldn't be together at some point in the future. If she got married to another person and moved away somewhere, that didn't mean that some day we wouldn't be together. For better or for worse we were meant to spend a part of our lives together. Two of the most important things in life are timing and patience. You have got to learn to be patient enough to wait for the right timing. Had I pushed the relationship at a time when she wasn't ready to experience the feelings I was asking for, it could have been a disaster. Our culture is very impatient. We have become a very "I have to have it right now or else" kind of environment. You have to train yourself to take a breath and relax. When you rush you tend to screw up and that could cost you a regret for the rest of your life.

It would not be an exaggeration to say that your mom changed my life in many different ways. I was told the secret to happiness in life regarding your career was to find something you enjoy doing and get paid at it. I saw a movie once about stuntmen and I was fascinated. The thought of jumping off a building or crashing a car and getting paid for it couldn't be better. The reality is that it is an unappreciated art form that requires more brains than guts. Even so, I was pretty sure I could make a career out of it. I found out that the only way into the business, other than having family who were already in the business, was to attend "The Kim Kahana Stunt School" in California.

The application had been in my bottom drawer since the eighth grade. The only drawback to being a stuntman was that you could never really settle down and have a family. I am sure many stuntmen do, but I didn't think I could be comfortable with it. I never really thought about having a family, much less a wife. I didn't think I was the kind of guy anyone would want to marry. I had a very low self-esteem under a shield of ego and bravado. I knew after a certain period of time with your mom that I didn't want to have a job that would constantly put my life at risk.

The only problem was I spent most of my life wanting more than anything to be a stuntman and I closed my mind to any other options for career choices. I didn't exactly have many things lined up. I decided the right move would be to go into marketing. My dad always said I could sell ice to the devil. That plan bombed with the economy when I graduated from college. I ended up becoming a painter, a back-up plan I had just in case. I was never happy doing it and I pursued other careers all along. It seemed like every six months I was trying out something new in the way of a career. It is amazing your mom never left me.

Even now I am paying back student loans from my latest failed attempt at a career. It was just another waste of time and money. Meanwhile, your mom was the one who suffered because all along she just wanted to get a four-year degree, and every time she started, I would come in with my newest master plan and shoot her down. Her life constantly got put on hold. Every time she would make a plan for her future, I would go and snuff it out. Your mom even believed in God when I met her and I extinguished that flame as well. There were only two things I ever did right for your mom.

When we got married I insisted we move to Manhattan. I was going to be the "big advertising man" and take New York by storm. It didn't happen and I ended up working in New Jersey every day. I ended up abandoning your mom in New York every day. I left her with no car and no friends. She was forced to adapt. Within one year she had an amazing transformation into someone I didn't recognize. In the beginning of our marriage, if we fought she would announce she was moving back with her parents. Now, one year later, she was telling me I had to move out and find my own place. It was actually quite impressive. For the first time in her life, she was truly independent.

In our third year in New York she took another bold step. She quit her job and pursued her career as an actress full time. Unfortunately, she was between looks. She didn't look like the sex kitten next door, nor did she fit the mom role. Sadly, those are the kinds of roles available for women and the other ones are scarce. I am quite sure if we could have stayed two more years, your mom would have caught her break. Timing is everything and her time was yet to come. I am quite certain that as time passes on she will return to acting. The great thing about life is that it is never too late to start having one.

I have some final thoughts about this chapter. One rule I always try to stick by when it comes to revealing things was if people ask you a question about yourself, you answer it as honestly as you can. I am brutally honest about myself. I haven't come across a question I won't answer. But, if someone asks me details about another person, I tend to say, "Ask them yourself". I could have easily listed your mom's strengths and weaknesses for you to read, but that would have only ended up ugly between her and I. At some point, in every child's life, they look at their parents and say to themselves, "I just don't get them". As your lives progress, you will find out details about them that you never knew. Each detail will fit together like pieces in a puzzle.

Your first pieces have straight edges that make them clean cut and easy to fit together. Then you start working on the more undefined pieces in the middle of the puzzle until finally you see the big picture. It's that search for the pieces that make life worth- while in any relationship. I have known your mom for fifteen years and I would be lying if I said I have fit in all her pieces. Likewise, every time she got two pieces together with me, I redefined myself so she could never figure me out. So I didn't really tell you much about her. She is usually right and she is extremely street smart and savvy. She gets ideas in her head that are trend setting and ahead of her time. She was a natural athlete and she could smell a scam a mile away, so do yourselves a favor and don't lie to her. She will see right through it. Trust me.

CHAPTER VIII

ABOUT OUR DIVORCE

All throughout this book I have mentioned to you how important timing is and that we all are destined for certain things after fate steps in and adds a few twists. The biggest case in point is this chapter. The first time I wrote this chapter your mom and I were in no formal discussions about divorce. While I was in final rewrites the book got lost. I then had to rewrite the book a second time. Now she and I had already split up, so now you guys need to know about it.

Your mom and I hadn't really gotten along for some time and our split was eminent. In fact, when I titled the book, "Things I would want you to know if I died tomorrow", I was metaphorically speaking about my death in your lives through divorce. What normally happens in a divorce is that the mother gets custody of the kids and the father gets visitation. So in essence, my "death" is a sudden departure from your daily lives. But believe me when I tell you, I do what I can to keep a grasp on your lives and be as much of an influence as my short time with you can allow.

The big question is, "Why?" Why would I choose such a risky time in both of your lives to divorce your mother? The answer will come, but like in any discussion, there must be balance. So the first question has to be why did I marry your mom in the first place.

At some point in your lives you are going to be faced with the prospect of marrying someone. What do you do to determine if they fit the criteria of the "right" one? I have already covered somewhere in this book about the check list from dating where you accumulated likes and dislikes in a mate and when you meet "the one", that person will fit the majority of that criteria. There is an expression that "love is blind", and in the case of your mom and I, it was very true. Your mom had qualities that excited me. I think what happened was I was so taken by some of those qualities about her that I over looked some qualities that maybe should have indicated to me that I should have thought through our relationship. I can't point to any specifics, but my parents, whose opinion I have never appreciated or utilized, were quite sure she wasn't the right one. I am sure I will wrestle with this as a parent as well. To what end do you step into your child's relationship and say, "I don't think that person is right for you". In fact, the more my parents pushed us away from each other the closer we got.

All I can do is hope that this book will provide you with enough information to choose the right person for you. If you believe in your heart that the person you are with is the right person for you, then your heart will lead the way, even if it is into the fire. The only advice I got from my parents was to think before I jumped into the relationship. That's not really great advice if you aren't thinking clearly already. I can't speak for your mom so I don't know what she saw in me. You will have to ask her yourself. In my case I was fifteen years old and just starting to rebel badly from my parents. I was never a great kid but your mom provided me with a car and a way to run from my problems and my parents. Her father had given me a job and I was set. Over the course of the next seven years I was adopted for the second time in my life and I became the son they never had. Her parents, like mine, were good people who would have given you the world if you asked for it.

There is expression that says, 'Humans, are creatures of habit.' We prefer routine. Most things you do in life cause you to fall into a routine. Some people have it with relationships; others with their careers. I had it with both. Your mother and I got accustomed quickly to the routine. It is very hard to alter your routine. It requires effort and a commitment to not be lazy in regards to your wants and needs. Rather than settle, you strive ahead.

My career choices didn't help. I believed I was too good to paint even though it was a great job and your mom's dad took care of me. I pursued other things constantly. The problem was that once I figured out something wasn't for me, I quit. I don't believe in wasting time doing something that won't equate to progress. I didn't want to waste any energy. This was a great source of strain in our marriage and I am surprised your mom put up with it as long as she did. Fear is a powerful thing and after you spend so long with someone, it is overwhelming to imagine life another way. She now tells me I did her a favor and I believe her. I had the same fear about picturing my life without our relationship. There is a certain comfortable security in any relationship, even if it is wrong.

At first, our marriage didn't appear as strained as our courtship until the money problems started. Like most couples, everything is great until the money gets tight. The difference is that to the couples that really love each other, the money doesn't matter and they make do with what they have. Unfortunately, it wasn't the case with us. The career I went to college for was advertising and there were no openings for employment as a result of the lousy economy at the time of my graduation. So I took the easy road and went to work with your mom's dad. It was nothing I had to work for so, of course, I didn't appreciate it and I acted like a complete jerk. The bad news was that the money I was making couldn't keep pace with the rent and the cost of living with your mom who used to shop to make her self feel better. If she felt depressed she would shop. So married to me, you can imagine within a few months we were over our heads with bills. Our wedding was a bust and we lost thirteen thousand dollars. So we started our marriage in debt big time. Within a few months I got a second job and then a third job. If you added up the minutes, I may have seen your mom six months total in the first five years of our marriage.

As a married woman, your mom had more freedom than she ever had in her life. I worked from seven o'clock in the morning until eleven o'clock at night. I came home to sleep. It didn't really affect me much because I enjoyed working. Your mom adapted to being alone most of the time. She had always had her parents close to her so she had never been alone. I would actually consider learning to be alone, an acquired skill. Some people can never be content being alone, which is actually more of a problem than you can imagine. If you can't be happy with being with only yourself, how can you be happy with other people? So it went, I worked, she worked and we never saw one another and we were happy, except the money problem kept popping up. We never had any. After a few fights and five years we decided to leave New York. It was around this time that I began to notice your mom had started not caring about me as much as before. In fact, she was beginning to make comments like, "Some days I really hate you". I dismissed it as normal marriage woes. Every couple supposedly fights about money and I figured we were no different. One of our other marriage stresses was that we never saw one another. It was a standard "catch-22". We never went anywhere on vacation and we never had any extra money versus we can't take the time off because we need the money. So I was always working without getting ahead while pretty much destroying our relationship. I fought to stay in New York against your mom's wishes because I really thought she was going to hit it big as an actress. I encouraged her to quit her job and pursue acting all the time, but I think it wouldn't have worked if she had to commute all the time. You need to live there to be plugged in there. A point for her that went unappreciated, many things I did to make her life easier went unappreciated. She always considered my actions to be self- serving. "It's always about you", she used to say when in reality I was trying to make things better for "us". Unfortunately, I have always picked careers I didn't really care for, but I let the promise of money blind me. If it hadn't been for the credit cards we probably would have owed nothing. Everything we bought was charged.

We moved into a smaller place with cheap rent and it helped us to save a little. After three years and two births, we outgrew the tiny apartment. Your mom was going stir crazy in that little apartment and had plans to take me with her. She constantly complained to me. That was her normal communication, relentless nagging. But I did think about our situation every day. Our marriage had always been about stress. I don't think there was one time your mom could point to when she was happy with me. We had never seen the light of day financially and I think your mom thought I would become something better than what I was. She imagined I would become regional something, vice president of something, not just an average Joe living paycheck to paycheck. She used to tell me she was disappointed in how I turned out. She had always had huge expectations of me and I can't help but feel she thought she married the wrong guy. She called me a loser and told me my life had been a waste. She would support me on my efforts and then wait like a cat ready to pounce a mouse to tell me, "I told you it wasn't going to work". I think she let me start some of my crazy plans because she didn't care if they worked at all. I don't think she cared if I came home at all.

Our final move to try and improve the marriage was the one that clinched it being over. We bought a house in February 1999 and moved into it August 1999. I had been working seven days a week steady for over a year. As soon as we moved in, it started. This wasn't right. That was all wrong. Nothing was good enough and she was impatient as ever to get things fixed. We couldn't buy enough, fast enough. We just emptied out all bank accounts to buy the house and now nothing but perfect was good enough. The only thing that happened with frequency was the constant cry of how stupid I was because I didn't know how to fix one thing or another. I knew how to paint. Anything else that she asked me to do, I tried my best.

In addition, I got along with her parents ten times better than with my parents. It was a constant source of stress for me. I couldn't make the two sides get along. It was easier for me to exclude my parents completely from my life entirely. I was constantly working on my marriage and I didn't have the energy to work on both relationships, so I bailed out on my parents.

In life, everything has a cost. The decisions you make are going to cost you one way or another. If you choose one road, you can't walk down a different one. I worked sixty to seventy hours a week and then came home and worked into all hours of the night. Everything I did had to be rush, rush. It all had to be done over night, and everything I did or tried to do wasn't good enough or fast enough. My patience with you kids had reached an all-time low and I found myself being short with you. Kids will be kids and I never had a problem dealing with anything you guys did, but now when you started to act up, I didn't like my responses. I was almost violent. Work was starting to slow up so I got a second job to help make up for some of the money I wasn't making. I worked on the nights your mom didn't.

Then it hit me. The more I was away from your mom the better things were between you kids and I. My hostility towards you was brought on by my dislike for being around your mom and her general dislike for me. Comments like, "I really don't like you today" or "I really hate you today" came much too often. I could feel the contempt oozing off of her. Comments like, "That's the way it is and if you don't like it, leave". And being called "useless" and "lazy" made it obvious to me that I was stuck in a bad relationship that wasn't going to improve and honestly I had had enough of it. I can't speak for your mom, but I was miserable. You guys were my only incentive to come home at all.

I didn't know how unhappy I was until I had something to compare it to. One fateful Sunday I received my comparison and it changed my life. I had just finished working and stopped by the store to pick up some groceries. The place was mobbed. While standing in the checkout line I glanced down the rows of people and my eyes made contact with a beautiful woman. Normally, I would not have looked twice. I don't make it a habit of "checking out" women but I couldn't help myself. "Wow", I thought to myself. I was really taken back by her. I could tell by looking at her that she was a warm, friendly person. She was amazing. I could tell by looking at her that she was an angel. She had a glow of kindness that surrounded her like an aura of light. The more I thought to myself that I shouldn't be looking, the more I found myself looking. I glanced at her left hand and sure enough, she was wearing a wedding ring. I didn't want to screw up her marriage just because I was unhappy with mine, so I tried not to look her way. Just then, the courtesy counter opened up and I was waved over to check out there. So I went to her and brought her over to the counter with me. She only had soup and batteries in her hand. As her reward for coming out of her line into mine, I told the cashier I was buying her stuff too. As I stood next to her I felt as if I was standing next to my life long friend.

She thanked me but said her husband had sent her to the store to make change for his one hundred dollar bill. As luck would have it, I was able to make change for the hundred with what I had in my pocket, but I still wanted to buy her stuff. It was my pleasure. Every time she smiled at me time stopped. It was wonderful. When we got outside, reality struck me and I thought of you guys at home. I said good -bye and left. I didn't even get her name. I knew if I started talking to her I would never want to stop. She was a wonderful person. I thought about her all week and I looked for her the following Sunday, but with no success. I really thought I blew it. She consumed my thoughts. I replayed every moment of our short meeting in my head. The next week brought the next Sunday and I figured if I didn't see her again, then I never would. Fate stepped in again and we met again. She told me her name was Debbie and that's all I needed to know. We met every Sunday for months. We talked and became best friends. She too was in an unhappy marriage. I couldn't see enough of her. She showed me things could be different. I have never been happier than when I was with her. I wanted more of the happiness she brought to me. By February 2000 she was working where I did at my second job and I counted the minutes between seeing her. It became obvious what I had to do.

So over one emotional weekend I told your mom my feelings. I told her that we had grown apart and I didn't feel for her the way I used to. There are some things you can't force and love is one of them. I thought I knew what love was until I met Debbie. She redefined what I was looking for in a relationship and I was finally happy.

I need to share some final thoughts. I am sorry I broke up our traditional family. Neither I, nor your mom will ever stop loving you guys and now you have two households of families who love you. It was a tough decision but I look at it this way. If you came to me for advice, all circumstances being equal, I would tell you to get out of your relationship. I can only hope that this doesn't mess you up. Adjustments are not easy. I love you and you are constantly in my thoughts. Understand that our breakup has nothing to do with either of you. There is a tendency for you to blame yourselves. There is nothing you did to break us up. And there was nothing you could have done to keep us together. It wasn't about you, although I am sorry you are caught in the middle of it. The bottom line is, by not staying in the unhappy relationship I was in, I am now able to pass on my love to you without taking out my hostilities on you that kept building up inside me. Your mom and I are much happier away from each other and we will pass that happiness on to you guys. I will always love you.

Debbie and I are married for over one year now and although we struggle financially, we are happy. The day may come when Mom will re-marry again or even have another child. I don't ever want you guys to feel like you have to choose between us. You have two families now. Your Mom lives in one household where you get loved, and I live with Debbie, Brian and Michael. We all love you very much as well. You now have people that love you all around you and there is no more hidden hostility, life is good.

CHAPTER VIII

GENERAL ADVICE ABOUT LIFE

When I started writing this book, I wrote from the perspective that I could be dead tomorrow and that you guys would have questions of me that I couldn't answer. The problem is that the questions you may have may not come up for twenty years, so this had to be kind of timeless. Or to put it another way, I wanted to give you wisdom that would last you a lifetime. I tried to write on topics that people have been talking about since the start of time. This chapter was made to give you some sort of advice that I would want you to know. Hopefully, it will illuminate a path for you to walk on for the rest of your lives.

It has been said once that there is no new history, only old history that affects new people. So hopefully what I have written will still apply when your children read it. It has also been said that a truth is a truth no matter how you approach it. I hope the truth I write will be universal.

TIMING IS EVERYTHING

Whether you are selling a product, an idea, or yourself, finding the right time to do so may make or break you. How do you know when the time is right? That's a toughie. Even the best marketing people in the world will admit, (at least to themselves), that they don't have a clue. I can tell you that part of knowing when to do anything relies on you paying attention to details around you. The more in touch you are with what is around you, the more likely you are to predict the right timing. If you are out of touch, you are out of luck.

Part of knowing when is a good time for anything goes back to what we discussed about perception. Let's say one of you are out on a date and want to kiss the person you are dating, let me start by saying you don't ever want to ask them. It looks and sounds so cheesy when a person asks another person if they can kiss them. Timing will reveal itself if you pay attention to the details that get presented to you. If you are both focusing on the movie, that's probably not a good time to be making a move. If, you are in front of your date's parents, it would also not be a great time to be sneaking a smooch. If you two are out somewhere by yourselves, do yourself a favor and please avoid the party scene. Parties of two are much more fun than parties of two hundred. There is nothing less romantic than going into a party to see some person act like a jerk because his or her main goal in life at that time is to get wasted beyond belief.

Fate usually gives you two times to deal with. When the time is right, and not a good time. As time goes on you will understand what I am writing and identify with these words. I can't point to a time in my life when my timing was really lousy but I am quite confident it happened many times. Pay attention to life. It will reveal to you all you need to know. I have always said to others I feel a pull to do something. Call it a gut instinct. Call it listening to your heart. Whatever you call it, it's there for you. Just pay attention to it. Learn to trust it, that hunch will help to tell you for the rest of your life if the time is right.

65

LEARN PATIENCE AND GRATITUDE

I put these two together because the lack of both patience and gratitude have combined for a one, two punch to snuff out peoples' hearts. Without these two things there can be no kindness. Without kindness there can be no compassion. The world is becoming calloused. Peoples' hearts and minds lack the feeling that was once there. The events still happen that are shocking. Only people are less receptive to each event because they are covered with layers and layers of these shocking events until no shocking event can react a person's heart. Please make it your mission in life to be patient and be thankful. A thought to consider…The Hebrew translation of glory is to wait. Think about it.

I can't stress enough the importance of this topic. People die today from stress. The strain from life and all its pressures are too much to handle and their heart gives. Around here, one of the bigger sources of stress is driving. When the day comes, remember to say these words everyday you are behind the wheel. I have to be patient and thankful to others. I don't know if it has to do with where we live or maybe some people drive like jerks all over the world. People will do anything while driving to annoy you. Most of the time they have no clue they are doing it. I once made up a bumper sticker that read, "People who drive slow in the fast lane should be shot". We have a lane on any highway to the far left. Officially it's called the passing lane. The only reason for being there by law is to pass other motorists. Yet there are people who insist on cruising in this lane at barely the speed limit. Sometimes you wake up late. Or you just couldn't get moving that morning. Or who knows you may have a real emergency that would require you to break the speed limit. These selfish, inconsiderate, holier than thou people refuse to move out the fast lane and out of your way. They think they are self-appointed police people and that they are making the world a better place. When in reality, they are causing the person behind them so much rage that depending on the circumstances may cause the person behind them to do something desperate and stupid. This can get other people hurt as well. This is only one example but there are many.

Learn patience for you and gratitude for others. A thank you goes a long way.

LEARN TO FORGIVE AND BE FORGIVEN

I know this one is going to sound a little "cosmic" but here goes anyway. Everything that you do requires energy at some level. This includes not getting along with someone. In fact, it takes more energy not to get along with someone than vice-versa. When you get along it takes energy, but because you like the situation, more energy is produced to compensate. While you are busy not liking someone and exhausting energy fighting with them, you could be missing out on something much more worthwhile. It takes a lot of effort and energy to hold a grudge. Not to mention the fact that it's completely not worth it.

Let's say you end up starting a fight with someone. It doesn't really matter friend or foe. For the minute it may actually feel good to you. Your adrenalin is rushing and you just had a huge shouting match with them. Then what are you going to do? You were probably shouting things you didn't mean. Or even worse than that said some things that you had been holding back that you thought but knew if you ever said would crush that person's soul. I mentioned this in the book somewhere else about watching your tongue and what came out of your mouth. Many people should not drink because when they do, they lose the things inside their brain that prohibit them from saying dumb things. A fight often causes your brain to do the same thing. What flies out of mouth often times you regret saying before you finish the sentence and what does come out is absolutely full of hurt and pain. For a second, however, you will feel a rush. That was the other person's energy that you just stripped away from them. Your crushing verbal blow took away a part of their very being. I had a sharp tongue like that once and I learned to control it. Once a word is spoken you can never take it back and the damage is done. You have to waste energy fighting and you may get their energy back but it's evil energy that you don't want from them anyway. In our hearts, we are all kind and loving people. Let it go, whatever it is. Go back to that person and make peace. You are probably fighting over something silly any way. Let it go and forgive and an amazing thing will happen. All that energy you wasted on that person will come back to you. I told you it was cosmic.

Joseph Assante

EVERYTHING YOU DO HAS A PRICE

Think about this one, I want you to think about it often. Too much, in today's society, people don't stop to consider the consequences of their actions. It comes down to this. Life presents you with many forked roads. If you choose to go right, it just cost you the opportunity to go left. If you choose to commit a crime, it may cost you your identity as an honest person. This is not to say that you should not act but rather, know the cost and judge its worth and be confident enough to know that the cost was worth it for the rest of your life and know you have to live with your decision. This has a lot to do with what we have talked about so far. Timing and patience get you to this point. The decision your gut tells you to make is where the paying the price part comes in. I want you to consider the price before the action. My parents used to tell me all the time, "Think before you act". The problem was I had a thick head and some things took a while to set in. My Dad used to call me 'granite dome' because I was such a hardhead sometimes.

The first law of physics is that for every action there is an equal reaction. Sometimes life pushes you into a direction and you have to throw caution into the wind and go for it. What you have to understand is that if you push one way it can have an effect on what is on the other side of what you are pushing. I like to think I have something I call a good decision bank account. In it, I have all the decisions I was able to think through in a timely fashion and was able to act upon without affecting others poorly. I go to this bank account in times of stress when I don't have the time to think through my decisions and I have a split-second to make a decision that may change my life or the people around me. In life, do what you can, not to rush any decision but sometimes it is beyond your control. I go to that bank account. I look at how full it is at that time with good choices made. In a split second, it's all I have. Learn to build yourselves one.

70

Every day you are given a bank account with eighty-six thousand dollars in it. Tomorrow, you get the same but, the catch is, the balance won't carry over. A smart person would spend it all every day and get the most out of it, live life to the fullest and thank God when they do. Now, go reread the last paragraph and replace the word dollars for seconds. Choose wisely.

LEARN GENEROSITY

Now that I have beaten into your heads that time is priceless and should not be wasted, I am going to encourage you to be generous with it. In my life, I have never been rich enough to give money away to those in need, but if I see a person in need, I try to help as much as I can. I once won the National Award for Outstanding Community Service. Every day, I would go down to a community center and volunteer tutoring small children. I hardly consider myself a teacher, but I did the best I could and it was one of the most rewarding times in my life. It was an experience that I could not have paid for anywhere.

Many people do not want to give of themselves. I understand because in life, there are going to be many things you want to get done but it always seems like you don't have the time to do. I was fortunate that I was able to make the time after I was done with college for that day. Everything has a price though. I really wanted initially to play on the college Baseball team. I originally found the Community Development Center by accident. Although looking back to those days I realize now there is no such thing. The college I went to had a nice neighborhood to the right that everyone shopped in and hung out in. And to the left was a side of town that time had forgotten that no one wanted to go into at night. I felt a pull to go downtown where nobody went. I found a charming pool hall, some nice stores and The Center. The Center had originally been set up in the mid-seventies to help the community. When times got tougher for the community. The center was receiving less and less money from the government. They needed help. So I showed up there everyday and helped out where I could. I taught the kids what I could. I went back to the college and had Toy drives, food drives you name it. For once in my life, I made a difference in somebody else's life besides mine. Be generous with yourselves. The reward won't look so good at that time but I assure you whatever you put out in energy will come back to you ten-fold.

I was once taught that the way to cure society's ills was not to take on society, but rather, find one person, focus on their quality of life. As you improve their life, it will then trickle down to those around them. Before long by helping just one, you have helped many.

DON'T LET POSSESSIONS POSSESS YOU

Too often in today's society we get caught up with having new, new, new. Before long we end up in a ton of debt, and if we lost a month of work, we would be out on the street. I have never appreciated money enough to save a lot of it. I don't like material things. When we live for our material things we lose a sense of who we are. When you fight with someone you lose your energy. When we waste our energy hating or despising someone this is no different. We waste our time living for the thing we want to possess. Let me say that I don't want to confuse things we need versus things we want to possess. You need a home to live in. You may not 'need' a small mansion. You may spend all your days and nights working to pay the mortgage on a house that you are never there to appreciate it anyway. That's what I am talking about. Everything has a price. You have to able to say to yourself honestly, 'If I lost everything tomorrow I would still be happy'. Many people today, could not say that and mean it.

The problem is that someone could make you do something that would compromise your values for fear of losing that material item if you get too hung up over it. A few years ago, car jacking was the "in" thing. Bad guys would wait until a person was stopped at a traffic light and at gunpoint attempt to remove the people from their vehicles. Some people actually fought the bad guys because they could not bear losing their possession. So they risked their life instead. They could have not seen their families anymore and left behind misery in the wake of their death, all for a piece of metal and bolts that come together to make a performance machine. Was that really worth it? It goes back to the energy thing. It will cost so much energy to obsess over something. Are you really nothing without that item you are obsessing over? Will you cease to exist if suddenly that item is no longer there for you? Is it really worth it? The answer of course is no. You lived before that item and you would live after that item. You may feel the quality of your life will not be as good. But, you should be thankful you are alive. Nobody ever is. As a person, you should sit down frequently and re-access what is important in your lives or what you are wasting time and energy on. Chances are there is something in your life that you waste too much energy keeping there.

Joseph Assante

TRY TO LIVE YOUR LIFE DRUG AND ALCOHOL FREE

I know the first thing out of your mouths is going to be, "You did it, why can't we". Let me tell you why I stopped drinking on my fifteenth birthday. The problem I have, and now thanks to genetics, you both have is this. I was adopted and have no knowledge about my family genetics or predispositions. It has been proven that some people have genes that make them more susceptible to becoming alcoholics. Alcohol, more than any other drug, ruins more lives daily. So the only way to avoid becoming an alcoholic is never to drink at all. If you never drink, you never have a risk of never stopping.

As for anything else mind numbing, I tried pot a couple of times but it only seemed to give me a headache. I tried smoking cigarettes before and I thought it was gross. Cigarettes are also stealth in our society. They usually go hand in hand with drinking and social situations. They say right on the package they are killing you with each one you smoke. Yet everyone does it and parents will sit and watch their kids do it. Loved ones will watch other loved ones blacken their insides. A cigarette can have up to 500 possible ingredients in it. I once got a list from a tobacco company. It was unbelievable. The most staggering thing I have ever seen was a nice, red piece of meat that went into a smoking machine to be smoked. In just one day, that beautiful piece of meat came out blackened and shriveled up. I can only imagine what that does to a person's lungs.

There are three major problems with taking a substance to alter your feelings of reality. Number one. You don't know what you are putting inside your body and what adverse effects it could have on your system. You're not a scientist. You didn't make the stuff yourself in a lab. You have no idea what a certain drug may be laced with. A friend of mine and I once looked at some pot under a microscope only to find it had a purple coating all over it. What it was, I don't know. I didn't smoke the stuff anyway. And he, after that, never did again either.

Number two. Once you start something like that it becomes difficult to stop. Your body will crave it. You might only have the drug one time and the drug may have you. Even a drug as common as caffeine will give you a whopper of a headache if you try to stop drinking it. You could lose your job or your family or both over some silly addiction. Is it worth that small high to lose that much?

Number three. What's wrong in your life that you are willing to risk your life to escape reality? Think about it. Every time you ingest some kind of substance it may be your last because your body may reject whatever you are putting into it and that includes alcohol. The human liver does not process it. Ask any doctor. Taking in drugs or alcohol or even smoking is a quiet form of suicide. Eventually, your body will lose patience with you and go on strike. In reality, using drugs or alcohol is no different than putting a gun to your head with one bullet in the chamber. At some point that gun may fire, and if you happen to be driving or around people when it happens, you may kill others as well. Everything has a cost, right? Learn to be very afraid of putting things inside of it. You never know how some things are going to react. Look at poor Kieran who found out the hard way that he was allergic to fish. Who would have expected that? He almost died from a fish stick. You just never know. And when it comes to drugs, alcohol or smoking, the risks don't outweigh the benefits. The moral of the story is don't start anything and you will never have a problem. Be happy on your own. If the only way you can have a good time is that way, then you had better re-access who you are as a person.

Joseph Assante

DON'T EVER GO ON A DIET

At some point in your life you may find yourself in front of a mirror, naked. Your response may be that of seeing a big hairy spider, in which case you may decide a diet will cure what ails you. Don't do it! A diet is nothing more than a walk down a road of deprivation. It self-inflicts physical and mental pain to the person. Normally, a person will go off a diet before long because they really need to eat what it is they were eating as a form of self-abuse. It is not mentioned enough but there are psychological reasons that we eat the foods that we do. The whole notion of being in the mood for a certain taste is nothing more than a chemical need in our bodies that needs to be satisfied, either through the food itself or the food triggers a reaction in our brain that distributes the chemical we need to make us happy. A better thing to do would be a change in your life style and eating patterns. Maybe you don't exercise enough or maybe you eat too much after a certain time. For some, food offers an escape. It's a busy day, so you take thirty seconds to let a candy bar melt in your mouth. You need to alter your life style, not find peace in a diet pill or starve yourself. Treat yourself. Just use portions. If you do decide to cut something, don't ease off it. Drop it cold turkey, one hundred per cent, it's the only way. The sooner you are without the thing you crave, the less time you will long for it after not having it.

I know that I am overweight. According to doctors I am overweight by 25 pounds. I would like to know whom that role model they are using for me because he must be some kind of freak. I needed to evaluate my lifestyle in regards to what I eat. After going to a doctor, I have come to find out that my thyroid is not producing enough and my body is overcompensating. They have given me pills, and a large prescription for exercise. Kieran is going to be six and I have not been inside a gym since his birth. I have no one to blame but me. Since I went to the doctor last I have lost six pounds. I still eat my favorite foods but I just don't eat as much. Tomorrow is another day and I can have some more then. It is unhealthy not to indulge. The bottom line is to be happy. If you look in the mirror and are not happy, you are the only person who can motivate you to make a change. You can do it.

LEARN THE DIFFERENCE BETWEEN LUST AND LOVE

Without a doubt, one of the most confusing emotions you are going to feel is attraction to another person. Love is one of the most powerful forces in the universe for human motivation, and not too far behind is lust. The difference between the two is a thin line at times, and other times, as wide as the Grand Canyon. Love has no boundaries or limits and, therefore, makes it difficult to define. I am no expert, but I can give you my opinions between the two.

I don't know how it came about, but whenever I dated a girl it was with the intent that some day we would get married. Think about it. A relationship will either end or you end up getting married. As wacky as it sounds, it really narrowed down the process of dating. When I went out with a person it was with the notion that I could spend the rest of my life with her. Over the years I never came up with a formal definition of what love was, but I could tell you what it wasn't a little better. A date for me was a quiet place two people could sit and talk, not a party or sporting event. I never liked going anywhere where I was forced to interact with others. It interrupted the process of getting to know one another.

As for the difference between love and lust, I will try my best to explain it. In love, you are attracted to a person and when you hear their name for the first time it whispers in your ear for the rest of the day as you think of them constantly. With lust, you still think of them constantly, but you could really care less about knowing the person's name. With love, you would wait all day in the rain for just five minutes with this person holding hands and leave completely satisfied. With lust, you are usually attracted to one specific part of a person's body and after getting what you were after, you feel empty inside and unsatisfied. The greatest feeling a person in love can have is another person returning the love that they are offering. The greatest feeling a person in lust can have is fantasizing about the one they lust. Lust is an individual feeling, where love can be shared and felt. You can share lust for one another but, it usually is like a light bulb that shines brightest when it's about to burn out. Short lived. In most cases the fantasy is much better than the reality because the other person may not be able to live up to your preconceived fantasies about them.

One of the tests I used to determine love versus lust was this. I used to remove a person's physical attributes. If I was attracted to their looks, I imagined them bald and four hundred pounds heavier, different hair color, and without teeth. Whatever I thought the person's best five features were, I took them away. Who knows what a person could look like in five years. So a truth is a truth no matter how you approach it. Love will still be love no matter how they are altered physically. When you are in love you may see peoples' flaws, you just don't focus on them. Love isn't blind, lust is. With lust, you don't care about flaws or anything else. You want what you want and that's it.

I want to share a story. Once upon a time there was a guy who really wanted a girl. When I say he wanted her, I mean completely on a sexual basis and he did not really care what it took to get this done. As fate would have it, she felt the same about him. The two eventually got together. I won't say they made love because you need to be in love to make love. These two had sex, really good sex. They ripped off their clothes like animals and indulged in each other. They met again and then a third time. By the third time something had changed. The thrill was over. The two realized that their attraction for one another was based solely on lust and they really could care less about one another. The guy was left completely crushed emotionally. He was empty. His fantasy got lived out and now there was nothing more. After they finished the third time and were saying good-bye, he noticed something about the girl. He was really starting to have deeper feelings for her. He imagined not seeing her anymore and suddenly a feeling of sadness overwhelmed him. Can we still go out from time to time? He asked her almost desperately. "No", she responded. He had blown it. She was using him as much as he was using her. Now he could never have a chance to know the true her. He never let her know the true guy on the inside, so why would she stick around?

Relationships are the most important things you will have in life and you should have some ideas about them before you enter into them. Good luck.

UNDERSTAND THAT THERE IS A BEST WAY TO DO ANYTHING
AND NEVER STOP LEARNING SOMETHING NEW

This, more than anything except timing, is the key to helping you succeed in whatever you attempt. If you don't accept that there is a best way to do anything, you can't look at the dynamics involved to improve on it. If you fail to strive to be the best, you won't be. In life, if you are coasting, you are going down hill. Accept this point and it will take you anywhere you want to go in life. A point that goes hand in hand with this is to never stop learning something new.

Most people get eighty percent of their learning before the age of twenty-five and make no attempt to learn new things after that. Even if it is useless trivia that you wouldn't use except on a game show, make an attempt to learn something new. As a society, we do very little to enrich ourselves with new knowledge or even keep our minds sharp. I was once encouraged by a special woman to write down something new I learned everyday. If the day brought me no new information, I was to seek out some new information. Not only that, I was to share my new information with those around me. It was quite a rewarding experience and to this day I still try to keep her credo alive.

There is a wonderful source of information in the New York Times on Tuesdays called the Science Times. You read things in there that don't make most news shows. It's really cool. I don't put too much stock in what I read on the Internet. I fear that anyone can hack into anywhere and write down whatever they want. The day will come when there won't be newspapers in printed words, only what is on the screen. Just understand that anyone can hack into a computer, and with anything, my advice to you is if you want to know about history or something factual, go seek out a person who has lived through it. They may be the only reliable source left in a few years. Anything else may be history re-written.

Even if you go to the store and buy a trivia game, do something to enrich your mind. Learn something about something. Your brain will thank you. The sharper you stay now, the sharper you will be later in life.

JUDGE PEOPLE BY THEIR ACTIONS AND NOT THEIR WORDS
AND DON'T EVER TAKE YOURSELF TOO SERIOUSLY

This does not mean don't listen to people when they talk. Some people give their word and do what they can, not to break that word. Others say "I love you" as often as they need to just to get what they want, but then don't act like they love you or treat you like they love you. A physical action is a much more genuine display of something than a verbal one. The more "all talk" you become, eventually you get to a point when even you don't believe you. Some people act and speak as if they are better than you. Other people, don't speak that way, but act selfishly. Worry about you and what you say versus what you do.

You are not God, and you are not king of the world, but often, life presents itself with circumstances where you get to play the role. Don't blow it. I have always believed that I wouldn't ask anyone to do anything I wouldn't do myself. No job was ever below me. Some people are too uptight about who they are versus who they think they are. Money and fame are nice, but I have already told you everything has a cost. Sometimes when you give in to being something you're not, you give up a part of you that made you what you were. Be thankful for what you have. Anyone can make a paycheck. Your actions define who you are. If you make the mistake of building your identity on what you perceive, you have. If a time comes when you lose that, you will believe you are worth nothing.

Joseph Assante

IN LIFE, IT'S THE LITTLE THINGS

Whether it's the laugh of a child, the smell of fresh baked bread, or going for a walk in the sun light of an autumn day. Whatever comes into your life that for just one moment pulls you away from its mediocrity is one of life's little things. It could be as simple as a smile from the right person that gives your life that little lift that makes life worth living. Take just a moment and thank God for life being so good, and thankful it's not worse. Be thankful for what you have.

The problem with the bigger things in life is the expectations that come with them. When the event finally happens, it tends not to live up to the expectations you placed on it. The little things just happen, usually when you least expect them. That's what makes them so nice.

Enjoy this book. I love you guys. Dad.

AN OPEN LETTER TO PARENTS AND GUARDIANS

In one of my many jobs I have had, I had the pleasure of working on a talk radio show. For those who don't know, talk radio is a lot of talking about topics that people are thinking about that week, as well as timeless topics that people have continued to speak about for years. At my disposal, was a "Talk" magazine that had listed the top thoughts people were thinking and speaking about that week. And it also covered timeless topics people discussed over the past twenty years. While I didn't think welfare reform or limits on political contributions would interest the kids, I figured life, death and things non-science would.

One of the more interesting things about talk radio is that it forces people to not only think about topics but, form opinions to others. It's one thing to have an opinion. Everyone has one. It is far different to test the validity of those opinions with others in an open forum. It's humbling to have a belief crumbled because you hadn't thought it out entirely as someone with another point of view states an obvious contradiction that you hadn't seen. Many times we adopt other people's beliefs without thinking them through clearly. Then we repeat them and look dumb.

The topics are not important, what is important is the act of discussion. The ability to discuss things in a rational fashion, with thought and interaction, using points to back up your arguments is what talk radio is all about. It's a lost art form that many people were never taught. I was very fond of a radio show I used to listen to on Sunday mornings called "The Art of Storytelling". For two hours, I heard four wonderful stories. For almost one year, every week I learned the art of making things visual through audio. It helped me to discuss issues with other people and helped me to demonstrate, through words, the points I needed to convey.

The problem that most of us have is that we lack the ability to communicate our ideas. We have no problem with small talk but when it comes to conversations with meat and potatoes we lack the time to map out and plot our positions on certain topics. This is bad. If you can't develop your own thoughts into solid ideas and concepts, how do you expect your children to? We are becoming a society that can't talk to one another, not because we wouldn't want to, but because we are incapable. As weird as it sounds, we have to learn how to speak and think. I am sure there are books and audio tapes that can help you form and shape your ideas for conversation but, like most things, the 'on paper version' doesn't always translate into reality. Probably the best thing you can do is to listen to talk radio. Listen to how people discuss current issues. Listen to how people back up their positions with facts and solid ideas. Listen to what not to do when trying to defend your points. This will help you in your quest to become a better speaker. For kicks, try calling in to one and tackling an issue. This is a dry run for the big show, talking to your kids.

TALK, TALK, TALK

Recently, on T.V., I saw a great commercial. A parent is at the morning breakfast table reading the newspaper. Their child sits across from them eating a bowl of cereal. No words get exchanged. Ten seconds later into the commercial still, no words have been spoken and a banner comes across the T.V. "Another missed opportunity to talk to your kids about drugs". I don't know that drugs is the right thing to talk about over a bowl of corn flakes, but the point still gets made. We blow opportunities all the time to talk to our kids. You're busy (work). They are busy (school). You both are busy together (after-school sports and activities). You have opportunities that get lost in your busy life.

Don't take this the wrong way. There is a time and a place for everything. After your child just scored the winning goal for his team and you are driving them for ice cream may not be the best time to ask them about the meaning of life. Choose your battles wisely. Timing is everything. It is no different than when you were dating the person you were in love with. You never wanted those times of "uncomfortable silence" and the funny part is, you probably never had them. Did you ever think, why? If you were head over heels in love, you probably spent most of your time thinking about that person. Even when you weren't around them, and were prepping questions for them for the next time you saw them in your pursuit to find out what makes them tick. This is something we need to do with our kids more. We need to think about them and their day and put ourselves in their place. We need to think of questions to ask them ahead of time so we can be prepared for our "moments of silence". Only through preparation can we calculate which questions will prompt the right answers to tell us what we need to know. The problem is, most parents are arrogant about their kids. When it comes to their kids they think because they brought them into the world they know everything about them. Let me assure you, this is not the case. Just because you are older and set in your ways doesn't mean your kids have their likes and dislikes are etched in stone like yours. Theirs change daily. I'll give you a perfect example that happened to me. I once ate a pickle and got sick instantly, and yet, my kids eat them without a problem. I would assume wrongly that because pickles aren't my style, neither would it be their style either. In the store yesterday, my son busts out with, "Dad, can we get a jar of pickles?" I almost fell down.

So, how do you "crack the code" when it comes to getting your children to reveal their deepest, darkest secret about their emotions, ambition, wishes and desires about life? Ask them. The secret is you need to know how to ask. Many times in life it is not what you ask, but how you ask that will receive the greatest response. There are two things that will make you successful. Knowing how to ask an open-ended question and actually listening to the answer. There are two types of questions, open and closed. A closed question elicits a response of "yes" or "no". "Would you like a soda?" "Do you think it will rain today?" An open question elicits a more vocal response and makes an opinion surface. "Why are those jeans your favorite?" or "What kind of food grosses you out?" or even "How are you?"

I mentioned, "How are you?" on purpose because like I said, the second part is actually listening to the answer. Many people ask,

"How are you?" a dozen times a day without ever listening to the answer. We block out the response because we really don't care. The question is, how many times do you do the same thing with your kids? You ask them a question and then interrupt their answer with what you wanted to say because you were more interested in saying what you wanted instead of listening to them. A few times of doing that and it's no wonder they don't want to talk to you.

TEACH YOUR KIDS TO ARGUE

I know you're reading this and thinking to yourself, "All they do now is argue!" They may whine and complain about each other. Maybe they may complain about their peers, or even you, but there really is an art to arguing. Probably one of the cooler things I took in high school was speech and debate. I learned how to back up any position with three points. A good argument can be made for either side. For example, if your child wants to go out tonight and their reasoning for going is because "Sally is going." That carries a lot less weight than, "Sally's mom is taking us so you don't have to drive. We are seeing a movie that I am also going to roll into a project for school and I get a 15% student discount." Do you understand? With 3 good points it made the argument very winnable.

Our society has lost that ability to discuss and weigh out the pros and cons. We live in a generation of small-talkers. As parents, we need to save small talk for work and have meaningful conversations with our children. Because we have brought them up on small talk, when it comes time to argue about a big issue, a logical argument turns into nothing more than a large plot against them. They can't see the bigger picture because no other conversation that you have had with them has led into that direction. An argument that lacks vision or a logical train of thought goes nowhere and just results in everyone getting a headache. Our children lead by our example. If we solve an argument by throwing a fit, so will they. When we start yelling when we discuss something, so will they.

AVOID PREACHING

No one likes a know-it-all. The last thing you want to do is come off as all seeing and all knowing. You have made some mistakes in your life, too. If your kids think you never fail, then they won't be able to cope with it when they fail. Along that same line of logic...

DON'T BE AFRAID OF HONESTY

Honesty is a good thing. In this book, I have come forward with some pretty revealing things. I am not big on double standards. I expect my children to be honest with me and I would hope that they would ask me things expecting the same honesty. I have always believed that you give people trust until they give you a reason not to trust them. If your child is fat, I think you should tell them. Part of being honest is having the strength and fortitude to receive that same honesty in return and deal with it. Teach your kids that and you will have given them an unbelievable gift.

DON'T BE AFRAID TO FALL OFF A PEDESTAL

On that same note about honesty, share with your children things that might embarrass you. Nobody's perfect. The only way they have to learn is through experience. If you have already had some of those same experiences, wouldn't it be better if they lived them through you? Instead of risking ruining their lives? Probably the only reason I never tried cocaine is because my dad shared with me an experience he had when one of his Navy buddies tried something like it once and died right before his eyes. Something sped his heart too fast and poof, he was gone. That was all I had to hear. If he had not told me the story, when it came my time to say yes or no to cocaine. Who knows what path I may have chosen for myself?

As adults now, how much information have your parents come clean on that has since enhanced your relationship? How many people do you know that found out some detail they never knew about their parents that had brought them closer?

For example, when I was seventeen, I borrowed my dad's car. Not just any car, his Cadillac!! I thought I was indestructible with this car. It was a tank. Anyhow, I was out joyriding one night and I totaled the car! After dealing with the hospital and insurance agents, my dad got a new car. From time to time, my dad would bust on me about the car. He even made me a plaque with the emblem of the car and the radiator cap for Christmas. I never lived down the guilt and I had always felt like I had let him down. Two years ago, thirteen years after the fact, he came clean. As it turns out, the insurance company gave him far more money than the car was actually worth. He made out on the deal! I carried around all that guilt for nothing.

It doesn't have to be something like that but I do know people who, as a result of finding out details regarding their parents, have bonded closer with them. It's as if they received a final piece to a puzzle they just couldn't figure out. Wouldn't it be great if they could have had that piece twenty years ago?

I think one of the reasons kids today think their problems and situations are so unique is because they don't know we, as parents, have had similar grief. Maybe they wouldn't feel so alone and kill themselves or others. Maybe they wouldn't rush to do adult activities or treat themselves so abusively with drugs and alcohol. If, they heard the consequences of those actions and lived through the experiences you have had that have helped shape you, then maybe that one piece of lifetime experience that you had, will change their view of you for the better.

SET A GOOD EXAMPLE

Probably one of the most important and hardest things to do is to lead by example. My dad has always told me, "Don't ever ask anyone to do something that you yourself are not willing to do." This one is a toughie. It forces you to look inside and face your flaws head-on. It comes back to the double standard thing. You don't want your kids to do drugs or smoke cigarettes and yet they watch you do it everyday.

I don't drink, smoke or do drugs. I don't drink caffeine and although with age and happiness I weigh a few pounds more than I should. I would not characterize myself as grossly overweight. I am not trying to win any awards, but I am trying to lead by example. Although my kids aren't even aware of this now, I hope when they become adults they will look back and say their dad was a good role model.

When I was in second grade, I had to do a project where I had to make a small book. On the pages, I was to write about my parents. Not being the greatest student, I of course waited until the last night to complete my project. The only time I saw my parents in the same place was at the dinner table. My mom, at the time, had created a wonderful meal for us that she thought a nice glass of wine would accent. My dad, who had worked a long day, thought a nice cold beer would be nice. You can guess what I wrote in my book after dinner. With crayons, I drew pictures of each of my parents and wrote the following, "This is my mom, she drinks wine. This is my dad, he likes beer."

The next day, after meeting with the school principal, both alone and with my parents present, I was able to explain our way out of trouble and a lot of counseling. A lesson got learned from me about what a child perceives and I swore never to duplicate that event with my own children.

Put yourself in their places. What do they see in you? Do you inspire them? Or, are you a stranger? Your smoking or drinking is no good for you, yet you let them see you do it. Do they see you smoke or drink or do anything that you would not want them to do? You would probably prefer they don't but how can you say it's OK for you and not for them? The sword cuts both ways. Save those lame excuses about it not hurting you if you do it once in a while or that you deserve treating yourself because you had a hard day. Save it for someone as dumb as you who may believe that crap you are shoveling. If you lack the strength to quit, where are they to get the strength to resist starting?

DON'T WASTE YOUR LIFE BEING A WORKAHOLIC

I was guiltier of this than anyone. I started working at nine years old. My dad gave me a shovel and told me to dig a ditch from a well he was drilling that day to the house we were drilling the well for. With both feet I jumped on the shovel. For a second, I was frozen in the one spot I attempted to dig into, then the shovel and I fell over like a freshly chopped tree. My dad just laughed and told me I would grow into it. At the age of 15, I held down two jobs. At one point during my high school years, I went to a different job almost every day. At the end of that year, when I did my taxes, I had six W2's! I have with only short periods where I haven't had at least two jobs. My average work- week is around 70 plus hours a week. As a result of this, I have really missed out on the first five years of Kieran's life and the first three and a half of Keaton's.

In recent months, however, with the help of my new wife, we have redefined together what's important in my life. So long as there is food on the table and the mortgage gets paid we will manage for the rest. We are working on cutting corners where we can. We are looking at our lifestyle and where we spend our money and concentrating on where we can spend smarter. Some sacrifices have to be made but, if that's what it takes to spend less money, so I don't have to work as much, so I can spend more time with the kids. That's what I will do. I didn't realize it was as bad as it was until it was pointed out to me. Now that I know, I promised myself to make it better. You have all the control you want, many times you think it is beyond your control but everything can be worked out if you commit to it. I was the biggest culprit of believing the sun would not shine at my job unless I was there to see it. I gave it my all at my jobs, so you can imagine what was left for my family.

There are two points of importance to remember. Number one, your bills will still be there tomorrow. I never took time off because I had this misconception that I was making some great gains on my bills. The more I worked, the more money I made and the more I got taxed to death. The more I made, the worse it got. Secondly, much of a young person's life is based on memories. Those memories really shape what makes them into adults. Imagine how good they would feel to see how proud you were of them in a school play or sporting event. And, if by chance, you saw them hit the winning run in or sing their very first solo, you would both have a memory that would last you for the rest of your lives. Do you think that anything you did at work that day would be nearly as important?

Think about it. We go out of our way to go on vacations with our kids, do fun things on the weekends, go to the circus, and for what? The memories. We hope that some point later in life our children will look back with fond memories of the places we took them. When in reality, we want them just to know how much we love them. There is no greater way you can show a person love than being there for them. You just can't put a price on it.

THANK THEM

One of the many things I stressed heavily all throughout this book is gratitude. To sum it up, without being thankful for what you have, you can't appreciate what you have. If you don't appreciate what you have, you can never be happy.

How many parents do you know that are constantly all over their kids? If they get a B in school, they should have gotten an A. If they lost the game by one run, they should have scored it. Every time their kids get a boost in one direction their parents knock them down in another direction. As parents, we spend much of our time being disciplinarians for our kids. We focus on a lot of the bad and not so much on the good. We constantly focus on what needs to be improved and forget the strides we have made with our kids to get us where we are today.

How often do you thank your kids for being good, or for helping out, or cleaning up? We ask a lot of our kids many times more than we ask of ourselves, and we say parenting is a thankless job.

DON'T BE AFRAID OF THE 'L' WORD

Due to the divorce, I don't get to see my children everyday. It kills me but, everything has a price and I always try to make the best of every situation. When I do have the kids, I make sure I tell them no less than 30 times that "I Love Them." I am very sorry that they got caught in the middle of this mess I have made for them but, I feel I would have been nothing but miserable to them if my other relationship had stayed the same.

It occurred to me yesterday, as I was dropping them off at their grandmothers house, and was smothering them with hugs and kisses, that if I wanted one thing to come out of "visits with daddy", it would be that daddy's house was filled with love and daddy loved them more than life itself.

I was wondering how many parents don't tell their kids they love them everyday. I am guilty of this only because I don't see them everyday and I have to rely on the phone as my only line of communication. Thanks to caller identification, sometimes my call may go unanswered. That gives me even more appreciation for when the call goes through.

Kids learn from your example. If you don't say "thank you", neither will they. If you don't tell them "I love you", they won't either. Part of teaching love is also teaching gratitude. If you aren't grateful for what you have, why would you show love to anyone for getting it? Kids are the worst offenders of this. They think vacations, day trips to the beach, after-school sports and everything else you fork out money for them to do is just part of life. It comes with the territory. If you're a kid, it's part of your contract pre-negotiated by some other kid once before.

They say actions speak louder than words. Kids today have one-second attention spans. In the time it takes to tell them, "I love you" the kids have only heard "I" and are on to their next project. To me, a hug says volumes, and it's a better second well spent.

Many parents are afraid to discipline their kids because they fear action will be viewed by their children as the parents being too strict, and that the parents will be viewed as the bad guys. What my parents used to tell me no to things. But then provide me with an explanation of why the answer was "no". Sometimes it provided me another chance to explain my side and re-ask my question, other times it buried me deeper into the hole I could not escape from. At least I knew my parents reasoning and I did not take it personally. I never thought the answer was no because they hated me. The decision that they gave me was based solely on them looking out for me. There was never any question about that.

The bottom line is communication. Don't be afraid to talk to your kids or they will grow up not talking at all. And, try to tell them everyday that you love them. It never hurts.

IT'S NEVER TOO LATE TOO START

It doesn't matter how old you are or your kids are. It doesn't matter how set either of you are in your ways. It's up to you to make a commitment to them and to yourself. Do not, repeat, do not come up with some grand plan to be implemented by you and then lack the strength to carry out your plan. You will lose their respect and you may never get it back. There is an expression, "The journey of one thousand miles starts with the first step". If things aren't right in your life it didn't get that way overnight nor, can't it be fixed overnight. You can be no worse off than you are now by building up lines of communication. Everything has a price and your kids are worth whatever the cost. Lead by example. The one thing I have yet to mention is this, show the people in your life your love for them every time you see them. It's not mushy or some sign of weakness. It's not something real men don't do. Sometimes people won't tell others that they love them because they are afraid they won't hear it back. These are your children. Not some person you just starting dating. The original premise of this book was telling my kids what I would want them to know if I died tomorrow, you never know. Even though they could read that here day after day, every person reading this needs to do the real thing in person. You can't write, "I love you" with a hug. Words cannot describe it. Get in touch with the love you had when you held that baby in your arms for the first time and that baby clasped your finger. That baby may have grown a little but it still reaches out. Do yourself a favor and be there for them. Find a way. If you think you can wait until tomorrow, just remember, something could happen to you and there could be no tomorrow. Do it today. Do it now.

Joe Assante

Joseph Assante

ABOUT THE AUTHOR

Joe Assante originally wrote this book with his children in mind. He pictured a young man in the Hospital on his deathbed. A horrified look on his face from the realization of all the things he will never get to tell his family. The young man wished he could write down his thoughts and review them so they contained all the wisdom he would pass along to his family if he were given a second chance. So that's what Joe did.

This book chronicles Joe's life. Joe hopes that by examining his strengths and weakness', his children will have a better understanding of the person he is and encourage other parents to do the same.

Joe hopes this book will be used as a tool that will help people develop their ideas into solid thoughts that parents can pass along to their families. Joe believes that many people are forced to excel at their jobs to support their households leaving a family of strangers in the wake. The book is composed in a logical, easy to read format. Joe hopes that the existence of a book like this will encourage more dialogue between families.

For more information, go to www.WisdomOfALifetime.com.

Printed in the United States
201859BV00002B/118-219/A